The Business of Sports Vol. 2
Making Sense of Diversity in Organizing Sport

The Business of Sports Vol. 2

ANNELIES KNOPPERS & ANTON ANTHONISSEN (EDITORS)

MAKING SENSE OF DIVERSITY IN ORGANIZING SPORT

Meyer & Meyer Sport

Editors of the Series
The Business of Sports:
Paul de Knop & James Skinner

British Library Cataloguing in Publication Data
A catalogue record for this book is available from the British Library

Annelies Knoppers & Anton Anthonissen (Editors)
Making Sense of Diversity in Organizing Sport
Oxford: Meyer & Meyer Sport (UK) Ltd., 2006
ISBN 10: 1-84126-203-X
ISBN 13: 978-1-84126-203-1

© 2006 by Meyer & Meyer Sport (UK) Ltd.
Aachen, Adelaide, Auckland, Budapest, Graz, Johannesburg,
New York, Olten (CH), Oxford, Singapore, Toronto
Member of the World
Sports Publishers' Association (WSPA)
www.w-s-p-a.org
Cover Design: Jens Vogelsang
Printed and bound by: FINIDR, s. r. o.,Český Těšín
ISBN 10: 1-84126-203-X
ISBN 13: 978-1-84126-203-1
E-Mail: verlag@m-m-sports.com
www.m-m-sports.com

CONTENTS

PREFACE

The increase in the sport participation of women, ethnic and racial minorities and those with physical and/or mental disabilities, the use of international coaches, and the interethnic composition of many professional sport teams are illustrative of the various forms of social diversity that currently confront sport organizations. Every member of society is continually subjected to changes that require shifts in sense making about diversity and cohesion. Individuals and organizations, including those in sport, are faced with the questions: "Who or what are we? Is there a 'we'?" The increasingly diverse and changing answers to such questions reflect a general societal trend. Individuals continually negotiate between self and group interests, between consensus and dissent, between teamwork and individual competition, between individual and group identity, and, between social positions and social structures. A key question is how those working in sport organizations and in particular, sport administrators and officials, deal with this increase in diversity in sense making and erosion of community loyalty and ties. The contents of this book, therefore, focus on organizational consequences of processes of sense making about and assigning meanings to diversity in sport organizations. An examination of processes of sense making in dealing with organizational issues means paying attention to the ways organizational members think instead of focusing on structures or systems (Weick, 1995). Organizational issues do not exist as independent objects but are created by people who engage in sense making. An investigation of how sport administrators and officials deal with diversity therefore, requires researchers to pay attention to ways in which organizational members make sense of a multiplicity of occurrences and processes.

The word diversity is generally associated with demographic or social diversity and as such, often denotes meanings given to groups defined by asymmetrical social relations of power such as gender and ethnicity. The current increase in social diversity in the workforce and in sport requires and receives attention in management literature and research and in policy development. Diversity can be conceptualized in another way as well however. It can also refer to a multiplicity of viewpoints and ideas that are created when individuals try to make sense of a situation or event. It assumes that individuals are agents who try to make sense of an experience or situation within a specific context. The resulting viewpoints may be dissimilar. Both viewpoint and social diversity are present in organizational processes, although managers, administrators and researchers usually pay attention to either one or the other. We contend that both need attention because they often overlap.

Social diversity can only flourish in organizations where viewpoint diversity is encouraged and valued. Members of a marginalized social group who wish to join a voluntary organization such as a sport club are more likely to stay if the club values diversity of viewpoints and ideas. This does not mean that all members of a social group are similar in their sense making. Not all members of a social group think alike and not everyone who disagrees with a dominant discourse does so because s/he belongs to a marginalized social group. A team of male footballers may disagree about more matters than does a mixed gender team. We contend that difficulties that managers and sport administrators may have in translating their rhetoric about diversity into practice may be due, in part, to their focus on only one of these aspects of diversity (Doherty & Chelladurai, 1999).

Dominant ways of assigning meanings to organizational processes may suppress 'otherness.' We therefore, address both viewpoint and social diversity in an exploration of sense making of diversity by sport administrators, officials, and athletes.

Most of the processes that are described in this book occurred in football clubs. This is in part because football is a popular Dutch sport with the greatest number of members and sport administrators of all Dutch sports. Football is also a sport with a diversity of participants. More boys are playing it at a notably younger age, increasingly more females of all ages are participating in it, and, immigrants of many nationalities are more often involved in football than in other sports. In other words, football is a site where those involved must make sense of various forms of diversity.

Although sport is a global industry, the ways in which it is experienced and organized, are contextual, that is, they are influenced by the local situation. Football rules are the same in every country but the meanings given to the sport itself, to the way it is played, and, to the way it is organized, differ across country and often by region/city (see for example Knoppers & Anthonissen, 2003). Similarly, although educational institutions play a large role in the organization and practice of sport in some countries like the United States and Canada, in others like Norway, Germany and the Netherlands, sport is played almost entirely in a club system run by volunteers. The foundation of these sport systems is the local autonomous sport club. This formal separation of sport clubs from other institutions such as schools and universities means that in a structural sense, sport can be studied in the context of relatively autonomous organizations. This local autonomy and its voluntary nature make sport organizations both similar to and dissimilar from other organizations. Dissimilarities may give indications of the uniqueness of sport and/or of the way meanings given to sport contribute to organizational processes. The relatively autonomous structure of Dutch sport also means that literature about nonsport organizations can be used to explore how sport organizations and clubs deal with diversity. Although the authors of this book use Dutch sport clubs as a source of data for their exploration of processes of sense making in sport organizations, their analyses yield various insights into general issues and dynamics of diversity in organizations.

The theoretical perspectives used this book also reflect interactions between local and global levels of sense making. The approach to understanding sense making in Dutch sport clubs is based on the work of Weick (1995), who is an American. The social group approach to diversity is grounded in American perspectives on gender, ethnicity and management of diversity. The perspective that conceptualizes diversity as differences in meanings or viewpoints is a primarily European approach based on the work of Barth (1969) in Great Britain and Koot and Hogema (1992) in the Netherlands, but also includes Joanne Martin (1992; 2002) who is one of the few Americans to approach diversity in this more European manner. The use of and interaction between these approaches yields a rich textured view of the complexity of sense making in sport.

As researchers, we continually look for new ways to understand the 'same' data. The data on which these case studies are based have been used for other analyses (see for example, Knoppers, 2001). The use of an analytical frame that explores both viewpoint and social diversity is however, new. In addition, our experiences in both teaching and in sport indicate that the themes and findings of the case studies represent various issues and processes of sense making that continue to occur in sport organizations today. Our hope is that the contents of this book will stimulate managers and sport administrators to reflect on their own ways of making sense of social and viewpoint diversity and will give them insights that allow them to challenge those ways of sense making that marginalize and/or suppress differences. Its combination of theory and practice may also make the various topics readily recognizable for the reader/practitioner. This book is therefore, intended for policy makers, students, researchers, and, managers with research interests in organization studies and sport studies.

Annelies Knoppers and Anton Anthonissen

CHAPTER 1
INTRODUCTION: WHAT IS GOING ON?

Paul Verweel and Annelies Knoppers

OVERVIEW: A SNAPSHOT OF A MEMBERSHIP MEETING

Last year two football clubs, Bunder and Donaro,[1] merged to become one club. Bunder had been on the verge of being dissolved because it had not been able to attract enough new members for its youth team. Donaro had many youth members, but its board of directors had been unable to realize its ambition to have Donaro's first men's team play in a higher division within three years. The two clubs had been talking for many years about a merger without making any progress. The town council finally broke this impasse by promising to build a new sport facility if the two clubs merged. The two clubs struggled to find and appoint a board of directors for the newly created club. The chair of this new board had no ties to either club. Two months later however, he stepped down for personal reasons. The board then nominated Peter to become the new chair. He had been the chair of Bunder and is a member of the new board. This nomination has to be accepted at a general membership meeting. The following describes what happened at that meeting.

The meeting is supposed to start with the reading of the minutes of the last meeting but they cannot be found. Those in attendance are then asked to approve the final report describing the previous year; the members however, refuse to accept it. A member complains that it contains very little about the events of the past year and is filled with personal opinions of the new secretary about the merger. After this tumultuous and disorganized beginning, the tension in the meeting begins to rise. The next item on the agenda is the appointment of a new chair of the board. The current board needs approval of Peter's appointment. A group of eight men indicates however, that it wants to form a totally new board. This alternate board includes the former sponsor of Donaro and John, Donaro's former chair. John has lost a struggle with Peter, the former chair of Bunder, about who has a say in the new club after the merger. John sees the alternate council as an opportunity to regain some of his power since the board of the new club needs new board members and has received much criticism from the members of the newly formed club. The current board, however, does not give up that easily. It does not want to step aside for a new board. A very emotional and heated discussion follows in which many old wounds are reopened. Various speakers refer to the club culture from which they come. They accuse others of either not taking cultural differences into account, of not naming those differences, or, of not forgetting those differences! The members of the first team threaten to boycott their upcoming match. All those present finally agree to vote to decide which of the two boards of directors will constitute the official board. After the ballots have been distributed, the meeting erupts in chaos because the exact issue on which the members are to vote is unclear. Someone behind the bar puts on the music of a popular Dutch blues singer ("A little bit in love") at top volume. The chair of the meeting gives up and dissolves the meeting.

SENSE MAKING

CHANGES IN MAKING SENSE OF DUTCH SPORT

What is going on? Why is this newly formed club in such disarray? Which processes of sense making and assigning meanings play a role in this struggle to create a new club? How do dynamics by which viewpoints are created and recreated have influenced the outcome of the meeting? How did some of these viewpoints become dominant? What role do meanings given to social group relations play in this struggle? These questions and similar topics are addressed in this book. The central focus is on the organizational consequences of processes of sense making about diversity in sport organizations. Since those in leadership positions play a crucial role in the ways in which an organization deals with diversity, the case studies explore the ways in which sport administrators and officials assign meanings to various events and to social group relations and the reactions of athletes and other individuals to those meanings

Historically, Dutch sport clubs have been social- cultural bastions in which individuals voluntarily come together out of love for sport. These clubs are not neutral places however, but organizations infused with individual, institutional and societal dynamics that are often assumed to contribute to social integration and, therefore, to societal cohesion. The societal dynamics that contribute to an ever increasing societal emphasis on individualism and rationality however, affect these clubs as well and indicate that this assumption about cohesion may not be valid. Sport clubs are under a great deal of pressure. Many sport clubs, some of whom are more than hundred years old, barely manage to survive. The meanings assigned to sport and to membership of a sport club have changed. "Loose ties" seem to be replacing unconditional loyalty and love for the sport club. Members are beginning to look and behave more like customers or consumers and see themselves as such (Anthonissen & Boessenkool, 1998). Athletes sometimes fail to show up for their matches. Competitions often erupt in disagreements between players, the referee, and opponents. Professionals are replacing volunteers in the clubs. General membership meetings, which used to mirror the democratic nature of the club, are poorly attended and replaced by meetings of committees of "experts." Clubs try to avoid financial losses by attracting sponsors and gifts from wealthy members. Clubs that wish to survive have to reflect on their identity, on the diversity of viewpoints within their club, on innovative ways of staying healthy financially, on ways to attract new members, and, on the possibility of merging with another club. Sport clubs are changing!

Some of the changes that occur in sport clubs are similar to those that occur in nonsport organizations. Most organizations also face the consequences of downsizing, mergers, individualization, professionalization, specialization, and of increasing demands on productivity. An understanding of changes in organizational dynamics and their consequences, requires an exploration of the context in which an organization operates. The authors of this book contend that processes involved in the construction or assignment of meanings to diversity play an important role in organizational life and must be analyzed in the context of organizational and societal developments. Processes such as immigration, individualization, and globalization increase societal diversity so that "old" ideologies and loyalties seem to disappear, and meanings given to gender and ethnicity change. Organizations are confronted with new types of social differences among members and/or with changes in meanings assigned to its primary activity, involvement and leadership. These changes must be explored to understand ways in which these meanings shape organizational dynamics and their outcome.

Organizational leaders use various assumptions about organizations to make sense of what is happening (Hylmo, 2004; Martin, 1992; 2002). If they assume that organizational members should have a unified view of events and of social relations, they will tend to strive for coherence and unity. Martin calls this an *integration* perspective. Administrators may also conclude that there is no one coherent view because each subculture has its own coherent viewpoint. This is called the *differentiation* perspective. Organizational leaders can also assume that coherence is impossible due to the presence of complexity and contradictions. This assumption of ambiguity underlies a *fragmentation* perspective. The deliberate and unintentional ways in which sport administrators use these three frames of reference to determine the manner in which they handle differences in viewpoints and among social groups. Their use of these perspectives needs to be explored so that interventions can be created that minimize the negative consequences of these meanings.

Nonprofit organizations, such as sport clubs, have to reorient themselves continually to attract and keep new members. This process of reorientation is complex. As the scenario sketched at the beginning of this chapter suggests, differences in viewpoints lead to new questions about power embedded in hierarchical relationships and to struggles about agreements made earlier. The results of such struggles influence who is invited to be part of a sense making process and/or to occupy a position of power and under which conditions. An organization's most common way of dealing with differences will determine to a certain extent processes of inclusion and exclusion of ideas and of individuals. An underlying assumption of this book is that these differences are already embedded in the process of creating the organization itself; an organization contains differences even before they become visible as opposing viewpoints and/or before individuals who belong to different social groups join the organization. This book therefore, deals with diversity in both viewpoints and in organizational membership.

The Need to Explore Sense Making

Sport and sport clubs are assumed to play an important role in fostering belonging and social integration in the context of diversity. Belonging and fitting in are essential aspects of life yet paradoxically, they are also based on making distinctions. Organization X for example, tends to differ from Organization Y. Citizens of a country maybe proud because they have the highest standard of living per person than other countries do. Similarly, sport can foster loyalty to a team and create differences by means of win-loss record and selective partisanship. Athletes are all called athletes but it makes a difference to them and their context if they play football or play chess or if they play for sport club Bunder or for Donaro. Mergers or the trading of popular athletes from one sport club to another can create ambiguity in loyalties. In other words, sport organizations continually undergo processes of integration, differentiation, and fragmentation. Dealing with diversity, that is, the inclusion or exclusion of individuals and of beliefs or ideas, is related to processes of sense making in sport organizations and in the broader societal context.

Sense making in sport is influenced by developments in other sectors of society such as in family life, the labor market and education, by processes such as globalization, inclusion/exclusion and commercialization, and, by social forces such as gender and ethnicity. Similarly, meanings assigned within sport as an institution often influence other parts of society as well. The meanings the media assign to male black physicality may for example, dominates general societal stereotypes about black males (van Sterkenburg & Knoppers, 2004). In other words, meanings are constructed in sport that interact with the way individuals construct meanings about difference in other parts of society. Societal processes may influence sense making in sport clubs in ways that may be unique to sport settings. The problems of old sport bastions and the concomitant increase in interest in sport by societal actors, such as government and businesses, interact in processes of sense making about and in sport by individuals. The manner in which integration (cohesion), difference (differentiation) and ambiguity (fragmentation) is given a place in sport organizations is dependent on the interactions among meanings given in the sport and nonsport settings (Anthonissen, 2004). Sense making in sport organizations is therefore, an interactive process among different actors and various social cultural forces.

The Organization of Dutch Amateur Sport

Dutch amateur sport is organized in a voluntary club (local) and association (national) structure. The relevant national sport association provides the competitive structure that is based on several divisions arranged according to hierarchical skill levels and by age and gender. The teams that comprise the top division are the best in a specific age and gender category. Teams that lose too many matches generally drop to a lower division. Competitions are arranged by region or district. Each local club usually sponsors several youth teams and adult teams that are also arranged in hierarchical skill levels and by age and gender. Each team competes in an appropriate division. This emphasis on hierarchy of skill levels means that most sport clubs encompass both elite and grass roots sport. The first team, usually a men's team, typically has priority in use of facilities and has a coach who is paid. The other teams that are sponsored by a club, including women and youth teams, tend to be coached by volunteers and have less access to facilities and financial resources than does the first team.

A healthy or well functioning sport club is assumed to require a broad base of many youth members and a first men's team that plays in the highest possible division (Anthonissen & Boessenkool, 1998). A successful (winning!) first team is believed to attract many youth members who in turn are assumed to improve the quality of the first team. This hierarchical organizational structure is often described as a *pyramid* (Anthonissen & Boessenkool, 1998). The elite athletes bring fame to their club and attract other athletes who wish to play at that level or to be associated with the success of the first team. The structure of field hockey illustrates the pyramid model. All the members of the women's and men's Dutch national hockey teams play for different first teams of clubs spread across the country. A national team is created a few weeks prior to the Olympic games or other international tournaments. The foundation of Dutch hockey success at the international level is therefore, assumed to be rooted in the model of the pyramid of the local sport clubs.

As was mentioned earlier, local sport clubs are voluntary and structurally autonomous organizations. The legal structure of sport clubs is similar to that of other nonprofit organizations. Generally, several individuals decide to start a club. With the help of a notary, they create rules that are congruent with those of the specific national sport association. They devise a name for the club such as Bunder and Donaro or using an acronym such as PTP (Power through Play). Theoretically, anyone is free to join any sport club although members often create a club based on various characteristics such as social class, gender and ethnicity. Rights and privileges are part of club membership (Anthonissen & Boessenkool, 1998).

Members of a club have a legal right to have a say in the way the club is run. This right is operationalized in the use of general membership meetings, one of which is described in the beginning of this chapter. Club members select a board of volunteer directors to govern and manage the club for and on behalf of them. Directors make and are responsible for decisions covering everything including policies for travel, the budget, the hiring and firing of coaches and other club personnel, and, the use of financial resources. A board of directors may delegate part of its governing responsibility and its tasks to various boards such as one that governs youth sport and/or adult sport and to various committees such as a bar committee, a sponsor committee and a finance committee. Their task is to carry out the decisions of the board (see Figure 1.1).

Figure 1.1 Organogram of governing structure of a sport club.

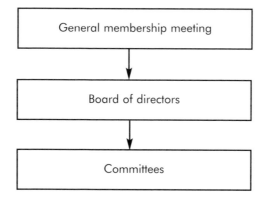

Every committee and board is accountable to the board of directors, which in turn is responsible to the general membership meeting for its actions and policies. The general membership meeting therefore, makes decisions concerning strategic planning and policies, the budget and changes in the statuses of the club. In the last decade however, the interest of members in attending these meetings has declined; this means that the power of boards of directors has increased.

All board members, referees, committee members, bartenders, chauffeurs, and cleaners are volunteers. In theory, everyone, regardless of gender and race/ethnicity, is welcome to volunteer because most clubs suffer from a shortage of volunteer leaders. The leadership of most clubs tends to consist primarily of white men, however. The terms *sport administrators* and *officials* pertain to all those in leadership positions in a sport club or organization such as board members, council members and coaches. The only paid individuals, if any, tend to be coaches of the elite teams. Occasionally, large clubs employ a club manager who is paid to coordinate the tasks of the various boards and committees. A sport club is financially supported through member fees, fundraisers, town/ city grants, sponsors, and income generated through use of the bar/cafeteria. Currently sport clubs organize sport activities for about a third (five million) of the Dutch population with the help of a little more than a million volunteers (Hover, 2002; Van de Meulen, 2003).

This manner of organizing Dutch sport is congruent with a strong societal tradition of volunteer work (Putnam, 2000). Citizens must take the initiative in organizing social activities at the local level. Local governmental support consists of providing sport facilities and subsidizing their rent. The national government limits its involvement in sport to encouraging the sport participation of disadvantaged social groups, to supporting elite sport via grants to national sport associations, and, to fighting negative effects of sport involvement such as hooliganism and doping. It is generally assumed that sport clubs provide activities that enhance the health of its participants and stimulate societal integration, that a healthy body contributes to a healthy mind, and, that athletes learn to appreciate and respect members of different social groups (Verweel, 2000; 2001). Dutch sport clubs therefore, play an essential role in shaping meanings given to sport involvement.

This model for conducting sport based on a club structure is more than a hundred years old and dates back to a time of communalism when many local activities such as choirs, bands and sport clubs, were organized on the basis of religious and social class divisions. Thus, various social groups defined by religion and/or class such as Catholics, Protestants, working class and upper class organized social activities for their 'own people.' The time in which these clubs were created has been called the era of the *pillarization* of Dutch society. Many such clubs were, and still are, shaped by traditions of family membership from one generation to the next. The contours of much of family life outside school and paid labor were, and continue to be, shaped by the involvement of young and old in sport clubs. This manner of organizing activities has given many clubs a specific identity. In the last 50 years however, individualization and secularization have begun to blur the distinctions between sport clubs while at the same time, the identity of such clubs is still sacred for many older members.

Sport reflects and interacts with societal dynamics to shape the identity of many clubs. Men's football is the national sport in the Netherlands; in general, men's sport, regardless of level or sport, receives most of the attention and resources at local and national levels (Knoppers & Bouman, 1998; Knoppers & Elling, 1999; Knoppers & Anthonissen, 2001; 2003). This is true even for hockey, a sport in which both women and men's team excel at the international level. In addition to gender, ethnicity and race also play a significant role in shaping the identity of sport clubs. During the era of pillarization, most sport clubs consisted of only white nonimmigrant men and women. Currently, immigrants comprise about 10% of the general population and 20-30% of the population in the four largest cities (Breedveld, 2003). The largest groups have their roots in Turkey, Morocco and former Dutch colonies such as Surinam and the Dutch Antilles; together they comprise about one million people in a total population of about 16 million. This influx of immigrants means that the social composition of many sport clubs, especially those in the larger cities, is changing. The social positions of club members in larger cities are therefore quite diverse encompassing old and young, immigrants and nonimmigrants, working and middle class, gays, lesbians and heterosexuals, etc. Ethnic minorities not only join established clubs but also start their own clubs, although in theory everyone is welcome to join. Consequently, as the case studies in this book illustrate, social group relations also play a role in club dynamics and impact interactions between athletes who play at the grass roots and elite sport levels, between board members and other volunteers, between women and men, immigrants and nonimmigrants, etc. Obviously then, sport clubs are half-open systems which means that their dynamics are in part specific to sport and in part a reflection of societal dynamics.

MAKING SENSE OF DIVERSITY IN ORGANIZING SPORT

In this introductory chapter, we introduce the purpose and contents of this book and provide argumentation why attention needs to be paid to processes of sense making in sport organizations. In the following chapter, Paul Verweel explains basic concepts and perspectives that guide the authors of this book in their analyses of processes of sense making of diversity. Since those in leadership positions play a crucial role in the ways in which an organization deals with diversity, the focus of the book is on the ways in which sport administrators and officials assign meanings to various events and to social group relations and how athletes and others react.

Chapters 3 through 7 explore processes of sense making in various sport situations. Each chapter consists of a case study based on a more extensive research project that focused on the ways sport clubs cope with processes of professionalization, merging, globalization or with changing gender and ethnic ratios. The case studies are not isolated or incidental cases. They were chosen because they best represent and illustrate the current and complex nature of dealing with diversity in sense making in the sport context. The descriptions of the various cases contain both the viewpoints of those being studied and an analysis of those viewpoints by the researchers. The first two case studies conceptualize diversity as differences in viewpoints or sense making. Anton Anthonissen (Chapter 3) shows how sport administrators try to justify the movement towards professionalization of sport clubs by changing the dominant discourse about the relationship between elite and grass roots sport, how this discourse is challenged, and, how board members cope with such challenges. Jan Boessenkool (Chapter 4) explores processes by which meanings are assigned in a new club that is the result of a merger. He shows how such mergers also involve struggles for power. Meanings assigned to sport and club membership within each club before the merger cannot be ignored but new meanings must also be constructed. What are the processes by which sport administrators include or exclude certain meanings or construct alternatives in the creation of a new sport club?

The next two chapters explore some of the consequences that the social composition of sport clubs and of leadership have for sense making. These case studies focus on the role social relations such as gender, race and ethnicity play in the assignment of meanings. Annelies Knoppers (Chapter 5) uses research on coaches to explore the extent to which organizations and sport are gendered and the influence this gendering has on sense making in sport organizations. Societal changes do more than nudge clubs towards gender inclusiveness, professionalization and/or mergers however, Processes of internationalization or globalization of the economy and of immigration, result in challenges to dominant ideas about multiculturalism.

Sport clubs are confronted with the incorporation of various nationalities and of differences between first, second and third generations of immigrants. How do processes of integration and differentiation develop and how are meanings about sameness and about difference constructed in sport clubs? Verweel & Anthonissen (Chapter 6) explore meanings assigned to integration and ethnicity within a sport context.

As we argued earlier in this chapter, meanings assigned to sport must be framed within their context. The impact of internationalism is not confined to sport clubs within the Netherlands, but also pertains to ways in which its dominant discourses interact with those in other countries. The relationship between projects in sport and international cooperative development illustrates the contextual nature of sense making in sport organizations. Boessenkool & Frank van Eekeren (Chapter 7) examine the construction of meanings in a sport project involving social actors from the Netherlands and South Africa. How do mutual understandings and misunderstandings develop and how do various actors make sense of these dynamics?

The closing chapter (Chapter 8) discusses the results of the various cases and their implications. Subsequently, the data and conclusions of the various case studies are used to reflect on dominant ways in which meanings are assigned in sport organizations and the relationship between viewpoint and social diversity. Knoppers and Anthonissen explore the complexity of sense making to determine which perspectives may help sport administrators and researchers in dealing with sense making of diversity in their organizing of sport. At the end of the chapter, the authors reflect on the contextuality of the results and on diversity of voices heard in this book and the role dominant and marginalized discourses play in processes of sense making in these sport organizations.

The case studies are presented in various ways. Some of the authors use a combination of ethnography and critical reflection to describe a process in a specific situation. Other authors create a synthesis of various studies to describe dominant discourses. All of the case studies are based on qualitative data although the data were gathered in various ways. The author of each case study briefly describes the context, states the research question, summarizes the methods used to gather the data, and, analyzes and discusses the results. The authors draw on literature from critical management and organization studies, feminist cultural studies and critical sociology to make sense of the results. The last chapter not only discusses the general findings but also reflects on the relationship between the researchers and the topic under study and how that may have influenced their ways of making sense of the data. Consequently, this book not only describes ways in which sport administrators make sense of diversity in their organizations but also explores the ways an emphasis on sense making can be used as an analytic tool by practitioners and researchers in sport and nonsport organizations.

Notes
[1] The names of clubs mentioned in this book are fictitious.

CHAPTER 2
SENSE MAKING IN SPORT ORGANIZATIONS

Paul Verweel

OVERVIEW

The purpose of this chapter is to sketch the dominant theoretical approach that is used in this book to explore sense making about diversity in sport organizations. A study of sense making about diversity requires an examination of the process of sense making. Individuals not only incorporate agreement (integration) but also difference (differentiation) and even antagonism and ambiguity (fragmentation) in their production and reproduction of cultural meanings. An exploration of the dynamics of integration, differentiation, and fragmentation provides a starting point for describing and understanding dimensions of sense making within organizations. The reader is first invited to listen to athletes as they interact with each other to assign meanings to the just completed match.

MAKING SENSE OF A FOOTBALL MATCH

THE THIRD HALF

The fifth senior men's team of the FSFC (Faster & Stronger Football Club) has just completed their match. After showering, the athletes take their places around a large square table. The initial fatigue of the match has been washed away with a first round of soft drinks and beer. The men begin to reflect on and replay the match. This is part of a tradition that in most clubs is called 'the Third Half'.

Pete gets teased about an incident in which he prevented his team from scoring by kicking the ball away from the opponent's goal. This incident not only results in a lot of teasing but also in reminiscing about a similar situation involving Martin a few matches ago. They also note that Tony played poorly tending to pass the ball to opponents instead of team mates.

> *John:* By the way, where is Tony?

> *Hank:* He really regretted the way he played. Normally he can take criticism but he got angry when you said that he seemed to be playing for the opponents. He went home because he had to do some shopping.

> *Paul:* Shopping???!!!! No athlete goes to town on Saturday to shop with his wife and the rest of the world. Saturday is for football!

John: You are right. Saturday is the day to be on the football field. We may have lost with a score of 5-1 but we don't spend time vandalizing bus shelters. Still, I am upset that we lost so badly.

Bas leaves the group for a while to go sit with the other team because he went to school with one of them. This action also results in comments.

Hank: Hey, wait a minute!! Do you belong to our team or to them, Bas???

The others continue to talk about the game including an incident in which a penalty shot ricocheted from the net post against the head of the goalie and into the goal.

They tease Paul because he drinks coke while the others drink beer. Their talk then moves to the next season.

Jake: Hey guys, I have to submit a list of who will play on this team next year. Everyone right?

John: I want to play as long as we only get players who can play. If we lose a few of the current players then only those who have played at the elite level can join. [Bas returns to the group.]

Bas: I am thinking about quitting the team. I have to go the USA for a few months for my work. We are opening a branch there.

Paul: Don't be crazy, Bas. You belong here. Do you want to spend the rest of your Saturdays shopping downtown???!!! I have to go to the USA for a month also and will continue to play. You cannot desert the team.

Pete: A few guys at work want to start their own team at another club. They asked me to join.

Paul: You aren't going to desert us for another club, are you? How long have you been a member here?

Bas: Hey, will Tony continue to play? He often has to work weekends in his new job and his wife has been sick several times lately.

Paul: That is probably the reason why he played so badly today but normally we need him. Tony is a good guy. Too bad he never stays around after a game but still . . ..

Jake: Guys, another round.

John: This is really the last one, Jake.

Their talk then shifts to the way Paul interacts with the referee

Paul: The referee is bad and believes everything the opponents tell him.. He probably learned the rules by taking a correspondence course.

John: Paul, you know that the referee determines the limits of how far you can go. If you talk nicely to him, he won't call you on rule violations so often. You however, keep commenting on his calls; no wonder he whistles against you so often.

Paul: Listen, John, that dummy has to know the rules.

Paul: describes an incident in which the opposing midfielder ran into and over him.

Paul: What that midfielder did . . . if someone from our team would do something like that . . . I would stop playing.

Bas: Me too. That midfielder is blind . . . it is terrible to have such a guy on the field. I think that even his team mates are ashamed of him.

Paul: But of course, they didn't say anything and just played on.

Hank then reminds Paul that last year he fell down in the penalty area. Since the referee thought Paul was pushed, the team was awarded a penalty kick with which they scored the winning point of the championship.

Hank: Listen to yourself. Five years ago, we were champions because you fell down in the penalty area. I thought you would never stand up again.

John: The opponents were so angry with us that that almost happened.

Paul: Wow, those guys of the opposing team were really upset . . . but it was more fatigue that made me fall than anything else, I think. I think I am going home.

After two more rounds, they leave and go home because Casey, the bartender, closes the bar.

The Stories that Are Told

Although the Third Half occupies only two pages in this book, it could probably fill several volumes over the course of a season.

The Third Half contains several stories varying in content and function.

1) There is the story about the mistake Martin made a few games ago. Pete's feat enables them to recall a memory that includes Martin again.

2) Pete's mistake brings disappointment but gives a new story for the future.
3) Their talk about shopping, work obligations, and the destruction of bus stops introduces the broader societal context in which the match takes place.

4) The discussion of Pete's penalty shows that although everyone is disappointed in the loss, Pete can laugh at himself. Hank's remark makes the penalty acceptable but Pete is not allowed to enjoy his penalty because the team has lost.

5) Drinking and eating together is an important group happening that strengthens a sense of group identity. The reactions to Paul's coke implicitly suggest that football players are beer drinkers. At the same time, Paul's persistence in drinking coke challenges that norm. He is allowed to drink coke because he is part of the team.

6) Mechanisms of exclusion and inclusion become visible in the discussion about the continuation of the team the following season. Although current members are getting on in age and their own skill level is average, only skilled new players are welcome. The ties among the members (inclusion) are also confirmed because those who do not want to continue are threatened with having to go shopping instead.

7) The remarks about shopping and beer/coke drinking suggest that these men have defined what is acceptable behavior for a football player and what differentiates them from women and from men who seem to be dominated by women.

8) The discussion about the rules shows how meanings given to actions are continually reconstructed during the game and afterwards. Not the rules themselves but the interactions with the referee and with opponents are decisive for these players. The football players delineate acceptable boundaries for behavior on the field by pointing to the unacceptable behavior of the opposing midfielder.

These men are all nonimmigrants and come from a variety of backgrounds (from Christian to atheist, from liberal to communist, from car mechanic to professor, from bachelor to father with four children). This means that they bring various contexts to the match. The sport skills of the players dominate during the actual match. In the Third Half, recollections of those skills and their contribution to individual and social meanings dominate the interactions among the players. Various communication styles are used to accomplish this sense making. At times, a joke or humor is used to get the message across. The discussion has primarily a teasing tone but continually shifts between joking and seriousness.

The discussion in the Third Half does not have a general theme. Several existing meanings are reproduced and new meanings are constructed. Game situations stimulate production and reproduction of meanings that extend beyond the actual game. The Third Half fulfills several functions/ purposes simultaneously. It strengthens the relationships between these athletes and includes other areas of life that mean much to them. Different topics and the ritual of buying another round are used to renegotiate team feelings and the different roles players have in that. Being together before leaving the sport world enables the athletes to absorb the outcome of a game. They can share the various experiences in the match with their teammates who understand them while at the same time they do not have to agree with each other. The implicit rules are reinforced about who belongs and who does not and which behaviors are acceptable. Nonsport experiences such as shopping, destruction of bus stops and paid work, are woven into the talk about the way the men experience sport, the team, and the club. The Third Half is used throughout this chapter as an illustration of the theoretical approach of the book.

SENSE MAKING

CONSTRUCTING MEANINGS

Individuals continually engage in sense making. Weick (1995) describes the actual process of sense making as follows:

> They (people) pull words from vocabularies of predecessors and make sense using tradition. They pull words from vocabularies of sequence and experience and make sense of using such narratives. But all of these words that matter invariably come up short. They impose discrete labels on subject matter that is continuous.... Words approximate the territory; they never map it perfectly (p. 107).

The assignment of meanings to new experiences is an ongoing process as individuals try to make sense of their experiences. It is a continuous process that can only be understood in the context in which meanings are produced. According to Weick (1995):

> Sense making starts with three elements: a frame, a cue and a connection...frames and cues can be thought of as vocabularies in which words that are more abstract (frames) include and point to other less abstract words (cues) that become sensible in the context created by the more inclusive words. Meaning within the vocabularies is relational. A cue in a frame is what makes sense not the cue alone or the frame alone (p. 110).

Frames emerge from a human need to try to bring order out of the chaos of impressions (Weick, 1995). Individuals and groups create and use a variety of frames for sense making. The Dutch, for example, have a refined system for categorizing rain, the Inuit for snow, and, others for the color green. Those words make sense in the context for which they were created. The statement of a football coach that "football is war" is an attempt to create a frame in which rules can be violated to ensure a victory. Football, however, is not war and violations are violations except for individuals who define a match as a war. Understandings of new experiences are pre-structured by already existing meanings and frames since there is no pre-discursive reality (see also du Gay, 1997). This means that the logic used to explain decisions and activities is constructed after the fact. The past and the present are therefore, connected. For example, the image of the great cyclist Eddy Merkx and the definition of a sport hero were reconstructed when Lance Armstrong won the Tour de France for the sixth time. The accomplishments of Eddy Merkx are needed to frame Lance Armstrong as a sports hero. Weick (1995) describes how this connection between the past and present works:

> Frames tend to be moments of past socialization and cues tend to be present moment of experience. Meaning is created when individuals can construct a relation between

these two moments. This means that the content of sense making is to be found in the frames and categories that summarize past experience, in the cues and labels that snare specific present moments of experience, and in the way these two settings of experience are connected (p. 111).

Individuals use cues, frames and interactions to assign meanings to their material and mental worlds. They also assign a value to these viewpoints by making some dominant and self evident (hegemonic) and marginalizing others, by creating formal and informal rules and regulations, by arguing for their viewpoint in their interactions with others, and, by embedding the dominant viewpoints in structures. This is evident in the ways stereotypes and joking are used to express and shape emotional relationships in the Third Half. Bas is loyal to his team and also to someone from his past. Hank's question to Bas about his loyalty reveals an implicit norm for team membership.

The men clarify what they understand to be good and bad behavior, who belongs and who does not, and, what is desirable and what is not. Sense making through interactions is also a process of exercising power since some meanings become dominant and others do not. The results of sense making therefore, reflect power differentials between groups and among individuals as well as practices of inclusion and exclusion (Fairclough, 1995; Ward & Winstanley, 2003).

Words impose labels on subject matters and together frame a discourse. A discourse is the major theme or argument of everything said, written, and conveyed about a particular topic. Although there are discourses that dominate, there are always alternate discourses, many of which are often marginalized. A dominant discourse reflects or creates a dominant ideology and is presented as common sense and obvious (hegemonic). Discourses are systems of meanings and often indistinguishable from social practices. In other words, discourses evolve from practices or actions and discourses give words and images that facilitate and institutionalize practices (Tolson, 1996). Actions or practices therefore, do not only follow words but the reverse happens as well. For example, a woman, called Melpomene, ran the marathon in the 1896 Olympic games although the dominant discourse constructed women as weak and not strong enough to complete such events (Cahn, 1994; Hargreaves, 1994).

This discourse prevailed for almost a century although more and more women participated in marathons. The material evidence that showed that women were able to run marathons helped to change the framing of the discourse about women as long distance athletes, so that eventually the women's marathon became an Olympic event. Subsequently, the discourse about women in sport became framed in terms of male superiority instead of female weakness (Cahn, 1994; Hargreaves, 1994; Messner, 1988).

Sense making therefore, is an active and continuous process in which words and actions or practices constitute and reconstitute each other. The changing of practices therefore requires changing or shifting discourses. Obviously, relations of power determine who is in a position to change the framing of such discourses. Social relations such as gender and ethnicity always play a role in this framing as several chapters in this book illustrate.

SHARING MEANINGS AND COHESION

Meanings are born in interactions in which events, cues and frames play a role. A feeling of inclusion or belonging is not only found in various and shifting forms of agreements in assigned meanings but also in the sharing of experiences.

Both the opponents and the participants in the Third Half experience the same penalties during a game. This sharing of the same experience binds the players and teams to each other although individual players and the teams may assign different meanings to it. Regardless of the degree to which there is agreement about the meanings assigned to shared experiences, the latter create the ties that bind people to each other. Being there when it happens is more important to developing cohesion than a shared view on what happens. Viewers across the world, for example, shared the experience of watching broadcasts of the same events of the Olympic games in 2004 in Athens. Yet these viewers may differ in the meanings they assign to what they see.

Weick (1995) argues that differences in personal histories make the construction of shared meanings almost impossible. Viewers of a football game may disagree whether or not a referee missed a call, for example; the disagreement and the shared experience of watching the game create social ties between them. This is what happens during the Third Half.

Although the manner in which individuals make sense of shared experiences may create significant differences among them, the sharing of experiences works as a powerful force to enhance social ties. Differences in the assignment of shared meanings in the nonsport world, for example, may be easier to accept due to the shared experiences in sport and vice versa. Shared experiences enable individuals to articulate and understand differences in the construction of meanings. Each recall of an experience ties a group together although members may differ in their opinions about it.

Consequently, each individual meaning receives a place in the shared meanings. These places or spaces are not necessarily equal as the case studies in this book point out. Some meanings may receive a more central place in the story about the experience than other meanings.

This means that there is a search for a shared formulation in many conversations that allows individual meanings to be articulated or be visible. The conversation of the Third Half is a good example of this. The situation and the history of the group determine the extent to which this formulation is unambiguous, contradictory or fuzzy. Athletes that occupy different ethnic social positions for example, may give different meanings to the same experience (Anthonissen and Verweel, Chapter 6). These differences in meanings become visible during interactions.

Constructing Organizations and Their Culture

Organizations, including those in sport, are the result of complex interactions among individuals who engage in sense making. An organization is produced and reproduced daily in material and nonmaterial ways. Ouchi (1978) and Peters & Waterman (1982) argue that an understanding of the functioning of an organization requires an examination of its culture. I contend that organizational culture includes dimensions such as the value attached to social cohesion, ideologies of dominant and subordinate groups, the degree of intensity of relations within groups, the extent to which behavior is proscribed, the institutionalization of proscribed behavior into structures, and, the processes by which some meanings become dominant and others are marginalized (see also Trice & Beyer, 1993; Douglas, 1982). Consequently, an exploration of the construction of meanings traces the relationship between ideas/ ideology and the ways in which individuals give them form and content.

Organizational cultures are recognizable in the stories of members of the organization. These narratives are usually based on three important themes: how things should go, what is important, and, who the heroes are (see also Du Gay, 1997). The stories also express the symbolic order, the facts of organizational life, and/or, how it is organized.

Tennekes (1995) explains that these narratives define the symbolic order in the why, how and what and describe those who belong and those who do not. Stories, such as the Third Half, define the individual actors and their qualities. The same holds true for concepts such as the Dream Team in men's basketball for the Americans or the 1974 World Cup in men's football for the Dutch. These concepts or words and the stories behind them describe who 'we' are, what 'we' are like and why 'we' are the way 'we' are. Such abstract concepts are conflated with social relations such as ethnicity, gender and class and help individuals and organizations to locate themselves and others in the world and to create culture together.

The continuous creation of meanings out of a set of events produces and reproduces organizational culture. Since culture is essentially social and interactive, its creation occurs during conversations.

The concept 'organization' is not so much explained in often used characteristics such as structure, formal goals, rules, prescribed behavior and production, but in the meanings that individuals assign to aspects of the social and material (re) production of these characteristics. The Third Half illustrates four overlapping levels in the process of sense making of a set of events.

- Individuals use words to construct meanings based on cues such as actions or symbols. These words are related to frames of references. The athletes in the Third Half use a specific sport related vocabulary to describe what happened in a game.

- Meanings are transformed in group interactions, that is, in meanings that individuals construct and rework with each other within the context of the group. The participants in the Third Half work together to assign meanings to their loss and the way it happened.

• Meanings are also embedded and absorbed into the structure of an organization and of society. At this level, the stories are not about individuals but about the occupants of specific positions. People are assigned identities according to their roles and positions. The referee and the opposing midfielder and his team are assigned roles that put them into opposition to the members of FSFC. They are defined as the enemy in the context of football and Third Half.

• Meanings are no longer associated with a 'knowing subject' (Popper cited in Weick, 1995, p. 72) but have become an abstraction. Abstractions such as *organizational culture* or *team goals* are however, never totally separated from the social group who created them. The remarks the Third Half participants make about shopping indicate that these men have defined what is acceptable behavior for a football player and what differentiates them from women and from men who are dominated by women.

The results of interpersonal connections at these four levels define organizational life and organizations. The Third Half reflects a pattern of interactions in the context of a recreational team that values both winning and friendship and in which social group differences do not seem to be salient at that moment. Yet differences in sense making do exist among these athletes as they do in all organizations. Bas announces that he wants to quit the team because he will be in the USA for part of the season.

His teammates do not see this as a valid reason and argue that if Paul continues to play although he is also frequent traveler then Bas can do the same. Consequently, Bas is not permitted to stop but is allowed to miss several matches. The interactions of these men suggest that they will go far in order to preserve the unity of the team. They continually resolve disagreements or diversity in meanings. The next section describes ways in which organizational members, especially those in leadership positions, cope with diversity in sense making.

COPING WITH DIVERSITY OF MEANINGS IN ORGANIZATIONS

According to Martin (1992), organizational members deal with diversity in meanings or viewpoints by using perspectives of integration, differentiation and/or fragmentation; different assumptions underlie each perspective and result in different processes of inclusion and exclusion. Integration (consensus), differentiation (differences) and fragmentation (ambiguity) each produce social cohesion but in different ways. I assume that interactions are influenced by the use of these three different but interacting and overlapping perspectives.

Every culture is marked by continually changing group interactions and of (dis)agreements in assigned meanings. Individuals may react to each other and organizational events by assigning meanings based on the three different perspectives. They may not always be aware that they are operating from a specific perspective; the ways in which they use these perspectives to achieve social cohesion may also differ within and across sport.

INTEGRATION PERSPECTIVE

The integration approach assumes that attaining social cohesion requires a central organizational goal, a hierarchical structure, teamwork, and, consensus. Organizational members accept a centralized authority and hierarchy. They work together to reach a consensus about the "what, who, how and why" of their organization. The resulting interactions and the meanings assigned to them are based on this consensus and are assumed to stimulate the cohesion of the organization. The successful production of goods and services is assumed to be influenced by degree to which meanings are shared. The more organizational members agree on issues and matters of importance, the stronger the cohesion and loyalty to the organization will be. Increased loyalty and cohesion are assumed to enhance results/productivity. An integration perspective is very popular among managers who believe that a strong dominant culture will increase the loyalty of organizational members to the organization.

This perspective is frequently emphasized in sport. Shared understandings, values, norms and ideas are often seen as providing a necessary basis and requirement for the success of a sport team. The participants in the Third Half, for example, reach agreement about the meanings assigned to incidents in the match. The integration perspective assumes that an organization as a whole has strong boundaries, has little or no internal divisions, and, can force its ideas on individual members. Martin (1992; 2000) and Koot & Hogema (1992) argue however, that social cohesion does not just depend on shared meanings but also on disagreements between people and groups, and, on ambiguities in relationships.

DIFFERENTIATION PERSPECTIVE

The differentiation approach assumes that organizations are places where struggles for power, competition among organizational members, conflicts, competing interests and dissent occur. Competition and conflict are assumed to be a result of different interests of individuals and of groups. Organizational cohesion therefore, evolves out of struggles between individuals and groups. The organization is assumed to consist of many subcultures that grow out of differences in or agreements with the construction of meanings and interests of the various actors. These meanings can be unique to a group and/or may also overlap with those of other individuals and groups. The organization is divided but the groups are not. The differentiation approach assumes that each group has its own way of interpreting reality, that the strength of group boundaries varies, and, that the boundaries between an organization and its context are permeable. The course and direction of an organization are based on short and/or long term coalitions between different subgroups.

Differentiation is part of the sport world as well. National sport associations and/ or local clubs may compete with each other for media attention yet be united in supporting the national team. Participants in the Third Half form a cohesive standpoint in their analysis of the game and the meaning of team membership but at the same time differentiate themselves from the opponents and from men who go shopping and/or destroy bus shelters.

The differentiation approach does not explain the entire sense making process in organizations, however. Martin (1992) points out that individuals organize themselves in small groups that are also based on hierarchy, consensus and team work. In other words, the differentiation approach describes actors at the organizational level but not at the individual or group level. In this post modern time, when the increasingly weaker ties within groups give individuals more freedom to act, understanding sense making requires that processes of fragmentation/individualization need to be taken into account as well as those of differentiation.

FRAGMENTATION PERSPECTIVE

The fragmentation perspective assumes that ambiguity and complexity of viewpoints occur within social groups and in organizational processes. Coherence is believed to be unattainable. The result of meanings produced through individual interactions has a greater influence on cohesion than do institutional and group meanings. Organizational members are presumed to possess a certain degree of freedom that allows them to reflect on and/or separate themselves from dominant definitions of their institutions and to be able to cope with ambiguities. A fragmentation perspective assumes that organizational and group boundaries are weak and that there are many ways in which people connect across organizational boundaries. Bas, one of the Third Half participants, looks beyond the boundaries of his team and sees someone who symbolizes his loyalty to his former school. Similarly, professional athletes may play for team X during the season and then play with some of their archrivals on a national team and against their teammates from team X. Thus, shared meanings are seen as fluid and as able to cross institutional boundaries. Diversity is not seen in terms of social groups or a variation of viewpoints but as a complexity of shared and unique values and backgrounds.

CONCLUSION

This chapter describes a framework for looking at differences and ambiguities in sense making and also suggests a strategy for exploring processes of sense making. An exploration of processes of sense making of diversity in organizations requires listening to individual stories and their intersubjective aspects, and, demands that different levels of meaning are taken into account. Frames, cues and connections occur not only at the subjective and interactive levels but reflect a broader context in the process of sense making. The approach to sense making that is used in this book presumes agency by social actors as they react to cues from their own past and from the context and use interactions to frame discourses that allow them to deal with diversity in their organization. The authors of this book assume that cohesion contains elements of integration, differentiation and fragmentation that are more like organizational and societal forces that work beside and through each other, than that they are categories that can be used to describe organizations. The case studies that are described in the following five chapters show various ways in which sport administrators use the three perspectives to deal with diversity in sense making in their clubs or organizations and the consequences of their choices.

CHAPTER 3
"THE PATH TO SUCCESS":
SHIFTING DISCOURSES IN A FOOTBALL CLUB

Anton Anthonissen

"It must be a pyramid. If you want the first team of the club to be at the top then you need many young players so you have a foundation on which to build. Results are most important. The first team of the youth should compete at the highest possible level to ensure that you have a foundation on which to build success" (chair of board of directors of PTP).

OVERVIEW

In this study of football club PTP (Power Through Performance) I explore how sport administrators change meanings they give to elite competitive sport in order to keep the club's pyramid structure intact. In this case study they shift from using a discourse that stresses the interdependence of elite and grass root sport (interdependent pyramidal structure) to one that emphasizes the professionalization of amateur sport (professionalized pyramid structure). The ways in which athletes and board members react, interact, and appeal to unity suggest that the discourse about the professionalized pyramid is a hegemonic discourse situated in an ideology in which elite performance is assumed to be most important (Knoppers & Anthonissen, 2001; Anthonissen, 2004). Although all those involved in the club subscribe to this ideology in theory, the shift in discursive practices means that the pyramidal structure becomes associated with inequitable conditions and a process of estrangement. The data illustrate ways in which board members can shift discourses to fit their plans, to marginalize a discourse that emphasizes 'sport for all', and, to increase their power to make decisions, and, in which athletes react to these shifts. The case of PTP is an example how an integration perspective is used to sustain a shift in a discourse about the meanings assigned to a pyramidal structure.

RESEARCH QUESTION AND METHODOLOGY

How do board members obtain consent from club members/athletes for a shift in the dominant discourse about the sport pyramidal structure? Which perspectives are used to deal with different viewpoints?

This case study is part of a larger study that explored diversity and leadership in voluntary sport clubs using observations and interviews (see Anthonissen, 1997; Anthonissen & Boessenkool, 1998). Members of a primarily white male football club PTP were observed during various activities of the club over a period of nine months. Interviews were conducted with forty members selected from various categories: board members, council, youth committee members, top male athletes, senior members, youth members, athletes who play indoor football and coaches. This chapter describes the part of the study that explores how board members win approval for a change in the meanings they give to the pyramidal structure.

THE SITUATION

The football club PTP is located on the outskirts of a large Dutch city. Pasture land, another sport club, and, a nearby highway, surround the facilities of the club. The sport club was created in the 1920's as a Protestant football club; in the 1960s, it became part of a multi-sport club that also sponsors tennis and dart throwing.

Football matches are held on Saturday because the club began as a Protestant club that did not play on Sundays. At the time of the study, PTP football club consisted of 250 members spread across six senior men's teams, eleven boys' teams, and one girls' team. Most of the members were white European Dutch men with a middle class background. Historically, the Christian origin of the club contributed a great deal to its cohesion. Societal processes of individualization and secularization have affected the club, however, especially in the last twenty years. Originally PTP was a family club, that is, children of members automatically became members. Currently that is no longer happening so that the number of youth members is decreasing.

Many youth drop out when they are about 16 years old because they have many other choices with which to fill their leisure time. Many work every Saturday which also makes it difficult for them to play. Attrition among senior members is also on the rise. Seniors members are not as willing to take on leadership and other volunteer responsibilities in the club as they were in the past.

The club's structure is similar to that described in Chapter 1. Since PTP football is part of a multi-sport club, however, the general membership of the entire multi-sport-club has more authority than that of the football club.

A council governs on behalf of the entire membership and is in a hierarchical sense, above the board of directors of the football club. I use the words council and council members to designate the governing body of the entire multi-sport club. The words board and board member designate the governing body of the football club and its members (see Figure 3.1).

The governing board of PTP football can undertake action but decisions about strategic planning and policies, the yearly budget, and changes in the bylaws require a vote by the general membership meeting of the entire multi-sport club. Attendance at such membership meetings of PTP has decreased so that the council and football board exercise the most influence on the direction of the club. They still must answer to the general membership however.

Figure 3.1. Organogram of multi-sport club

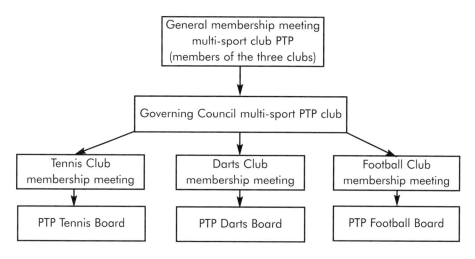

FRAMES, CUES AND DISCOURSES

FRAMING THE PYRAMID

The quotation at the beginning of this chapter illustrates how the organizational structure of the football club PTP was originally based on the concept of an interdependent pyramid in which grass roots and elite sport coexist and are interdependent (see also Verweel & Knoppers, Chapter 1). During the time that the research was conducted, the council of the entire club and the board of PTP football jointly announce that from now on the emphasis of the football club will be on high performance sport. A board member explains, "Football is a competitive sport that requires a high level of play/competition. It is therefore logical that we go in that direction" (Anthonissen & Boessenkool 1998, p. 73). Members wonder to what extent this change in emphasis reflects the wishes of the membership or of the chair and a few board members. A football player complains: "It seems as if board members are just looking for a new challenge but the necessity of this plan is not clear to me" (Anthonissen 1997, p. 6). The board is afraid PTP will deteriorate if elite men's football is not emphasized. A board member explains: "If we do not choose for this [elite sport] then our level of achievement will go downhill; then you could probably have fun playing football with each other at a lower level but then no one comes to the club house anymore and boys will not want to come and play here" (Anthonissen & Boessenkool 1998, p. 73). The PTP board and council want to make the club attractive to the youth members, to increase the involvement of members, to create better conditions that enable elite performance, and, to enhance club loyalty by attracting well-known football players from the area. They see this as strengthening the pyramidal structure.

There are ambivalent feelings among football club members about the benefits of having a professional pyramidal structure. Several boys who currently play for the club's top men's team want to be famous Dutch football stars such as Kluivert or Bergkamp and see this as a positive change. One player says: "When there is more financial support for the best boys, then the big clubs will send their scouts. That is good for the whole club and for us" (Anthonissen 1997, p. 34). On the other hand, several talented members of this elite team are not that ambitious and occasionally prefer to do something else on Saturday than play football. When they go to Disneyland on a Saturday, they keep the reason for their absence a secret from the team. Several senior members of a lower division team do not agree with the change in the emphasis; they prefer a discourse that emphasizes individual achievement. A senior member argues: "I come every Saturday just to kick a ball around; now I see the club going in that [professional] direction. I just want to have some fun with my friends. I realize that we need youth members to ensure continuity but to tell you the truth, that has always been difficult" (Anthonissen, 1997, p. 21). Other members of lower division teams say that although their teams do not compete at the elite level, they do play well every Saturday. Therefore, there should be room for them. Some members think that the multi-sport club council and the football board are innovative and visionary but also think that board members want to score with the accomplishments of the first men's team. This diversity in meanings assigned to playing football for PTP and to performance suggests that PTP club members and its board of directors see the gap between meanings assigned to elite performance and to self defined achievement in sport as a source of tension within the club.

Although one of the objectives of the proposal is to increase their number, the younger athletes also have a variety of reactions to the proposed shift. The boys to whom this emphasis on high performance is supposed to appeal, have their own ideas about commitment to the club. "I want to do fun things as well and do not want to come and practice so often" asserts a player of the team for 14-16 year olds (Anthonissen 1997, p. 25). Many male athletes seem to be more interested in enjoying themselves than playing in a higher division. Often, there are difficulties in assigning youth members to teams because some of them want to play together despite skill differences.

Senior club members have their own ideas about the possible increase in participation of these youth members. Some think that the enthusiasm of the youth to play football in an organized setting is decreasing. Senior members worry about the decrease in the number of boys who move from youth to adult football. They attribute a change in attitude in these boys to the influence of sponsors. A senior member explains: "They [boys] have it too easy; they first look to see what is in it for them. They do not put the club first" (Anthonissen, 1997, p. 25). Several senior members argue that a mentality is beginning to develop that places less emphasis on elite performance and more on individually defined achievements. These seniors often compare the state of affairs of the current club with "how it used to be". Younger members confirm this change in attitude. They see no reason to stay with PTP if they do not like the club culture, if the facilities are bad, or, if they move. An athlete who is dropping out explains: "My family is moving to a new neighborhood that also has a football club . . . then I do not have to travel so far to play" (Anthonissen, 1997, p. 27).

Members of the youth committee have a somewhat different perspective about the changes in enthusiasm and performance orientation among the youth. They see that there are still enough boys who want to play football at a high level although they also recognize that these boys tend to choose clubs with good facilities. Other youth committee members think that the demands placed on these boys are not always realistic and that cultural issues play a role as well. One committee member explains that "we have a few immigrant boys playing at the youth level. They usually deliver papers on Saturday, have other jobs, or, just do not come" (Anthonissen 1997, p. 18).

Obviously the board's proposal to give more attention to the elite players elicits various reactions from members. Not everyone accepts the shift in emphasis in the pyramidal structure. Yet the pyramidal discourse itself is not challenged; members do not seem to mind that attention is given to elite players as long as their own opportunities to play and the social characteristics of the club are not affected. Some members react to the decision made by the board by using a discourse that is framed by an interdependent pyramidal structure. The board however, goes ahead with its plans to implement the announced change in emphasis.

CHANGING CUES

Most of the club members learn about the implementation of a change in emphasis in PTP football from the local newspaper. The newspaper article reports that the PTP board has chosen to give most of its attention to the elite level men's team because football is a competitive and high performance sport. The board plans to hire a more expensive trainer to enable the elite team to play in the top division of Saturday football in two years time. The article continues to say that this emphasis on top performance does not mean that less attention will be paid to the recreation, girls' or indoor football teams. The chair of the board tries to dissolve a possible conflict between the elite and sport- for -all discourses and states that "other teams must also have the opportunity to develop their skills" (Anthonissen & Boessenkool, 1998, p. 76). The chair argues that "all members have to feel at home here; a feeling of solidarity is important to club members" (Anthonissen, 1997, p. 22).

Members of the grass roots teams think that the new emphasis does and will affect their teams negatively, however. They are unhappy because for a long time already most of the attention of the board has been devoted to the top teams and now it will be intensified. A board member realizes that some members think this but counters by arguing that it is easy to react like that. According to him, club loyalty plays a large role in this: "Feelings of loyalty to the club end about halfway in the second team; those who play at a level lower than the second team want to play together as a team and expect everything to be well organized. If it [football competition] would be better organized at another club like Sporting B then they will play there" (Anthonissen & Boessenkool, 1998, p. 73).

There are also members who do not play on the elite teams who are loyal to and involved with the club. An athlete argues that "being a member of PTP goes beyond my team. I wouldn't want to play football for just any club; that is not enjoyable. I like to come to the clubhouse after a match to drink a beer and to see different people" (Anthonissen 1997,

p. 22). Others are primarily loyal to their team but do not see that as a problem because they are also loyal to the system. According to them, everyone should be able to enjoy himself or herself and that means attention should be paid to teams every category. The debate becomes very polarized. Some members see the change in emphasis as a policy issue about whether or not to provide more resources for the elite players. Others argue that this emphasis will change the social character of the club, the assumed equality of players and teams, and, the decision making process. It will result in a culture in which decisions are made within a hierarchical structure instead of by members. In other words, many members use the discourse about interdependent pyramid structure as their dominant frame for thinking and behaving.

OBTAINING EXTERNAL SUPPORT

The football board continues on its chosen path and works to create more support by going outside the club. It establishes a Foundation for Elite Level Football that has to generate money and create conditions to enable elite level football to be played at PTP. The PTP board defends this action by using recent and similar developments in other clubs as evidence. A board member explains that

> We agreed to the professionalization of football. It was no longer justifiable to pay for the costs of elite players out of the general budget. We discussed this with board members of another big club in the city who have taken similar steps. The competition among the clubs is increasing and the KNVB and the local government also promote the idea of big clubs who work in a professional manner" (Anthonissen & Boessenkool, 1998, p. 74)[2]

The board tries to generate support by showing its discourse is supported by important stakeholders (the context). The board members appeal to dominant societal discourses about professionalization, individualization of society, and, the 24-hour economy. The proposed change in policy is therefore framed as being part of an adaptation to changes in society and to solutions proposed by the context (see also O'Brien & Slack, 1999).

Other reasons for creating a foundation include a plan to recruit in the new housing development that will be built beside the club, a concern for the decrease in the number of memberships, and, dissatisfaction with the performance of the men's first team. The latter means that more highly skilled players need to be recruited from outside the club. These arguments are also situated within the ideology of a pyramid with an emphasis on elite sport. Little, if any, attention is paid to the possible effect this recruitment might have on the current members of the first team. The goal of the football board is to ensure that the first team performs at the elite level so that new players will be attracted to the club.

Ironically, the current players of the first team show little interest in the creation of the Foundation. They are not so much interested in the resulting benefits such as free membership, travel, shoes, clothes and care and a nominal bonus of eight euro per point per player or position, as they are concerned about the arrival of new players from other clubs and the selection of the first team for next year. Being a member of the first men's team means everything to several players. If they cannot play for that team then they will leave to play for another club. They foresee that their position as heroes of and their ties with the current club may be endangered. The idea that the club will grow if they play at a higher level has little impact on them.

Besides creating the Foundation Elite Level Football, the football board also decides to set up a Business Club. This club is associated with the Foundation. It offers businesses in the neighborhood the opportunity to promote their products to other companies, suppliers and/or other potential customers in PTP's restaurant/bar. The paid memberships of the business club serve as an additional source of income for financing the men's senior and youth elite teams. Whereas previous arguments and actions of the board were congruent with the predominant Dutch club model and its accompanying volunteer culture, these decisions are in direct opposition to it. The general membership will no longer have the final say about financial matters and other plans concerning elite sport. This is contrary to the prevailing culture of the club.

USING EXTERNAL DISCOURSES

The broader societal context plays a role in the decision making process of the board members as well. They venture beyond club boundaries when they want to broaden the base by recruiting new youth members, to compare themselves to competing clubs, to look/search for sponsors, and, to strengthen the pyramid. In addition, they import a societal discourse that supports the ideology underlying their choice for a professionalized pyramidal structure.

Similarly, the council of the multi-sport club allows itself to be guided in its actions by external forces such as the building of a new housing development nearby and the perceived pressure from the National Dutch Football Association (KNVB). Board and council members see themselves as victims of external top down structures. One council member explains "that is how the system is; you cannot escape from it" (Anthonissen, 1997, p. 20). The board of PTP football thinks it has no choice but to raise the level of play of the elite teams and that that requires a higher level of professionalization than currently exists. These two factors are considered the most important reasons for creating a Foundation and a Business club.

   The various relationships the board has in the world outside the club seem to reinforce the resolve of PTP board members and suggest that the path they have chosen is the right one. This justification lessens their frustrations about the lack of involvement and support of club members. Furthermore, the large amount of money involved ensures that the feelings of responsibility and status of PTP board members increase. Although a few of the board members see this as self-serving, most see it as serving the collective interest of the club. A member explains that "if we hadn't done this, the club would have gone downhill" (Anthonissen, 1997, p. 11). The football board and the multi-sport council reason that this plan benefits the continuity of the club, a factor that impacts all members. A team that performs well in the first division is assumed to increase the base of the pyramid, which in turn will ensure continuity of the club and the other elite teams. They are not the only club to make these arguments, however.

Many national sport associations in other countries encourage the professionalization of sport clubs using discourses that assume and emphasize the interrelatedness of economics and quality (De Martelaer et al., 2002; Horch, 1997; Koski & Heikkila, 1997; Nier & Sheard, 1999). Similarly, the influence of a market economy on Dutch sport clubs and other volunteer organization is also increasing. The participation of at least one club team in elite level competition is generally assumed crucial in attracting sponsors. This assumption also guides the actions of PTP board members. As a board member explains: "We are talking about a partnership: for the club itself and also for the individual members. Besides developing a PTP arrangement with discounts on credit cards and mortgages, we are thinking about savings programs for members" (Anthonissen & Boessenkool, 1998, p. 86). The PTP multi-sport council understands that a large club is attractive to sponsors; the more members a club has, the greater the number of potential customers for the sponsors. It seems as if there is only one way of doing business. The market -driven economy is used to strengthen a pyramidal discourse that emphasizes elite level sport grounded in a broad base. Obviously then, board and council use social forces within and outside of the club to strengthen discourses that fit their objectives.

WORKING OUTSIDE TRADITIONAL FRAMES

WORKING INFORMALLY

A small group of the board members works hard behind the scenes to implement this plan. A board member defends the reason for their informal way of working. He says: "If you do not watch out, then everyone will have spent the money three times before a cent has come in; even those who recruit new players are already promising rewards for top performance. So we have to be careful" (Anthonissen & Boessenkool, 1998, p. 80). This informal way of working means that many members are caught by surprise when the plan is announced and implemented. This surprise reveals the gap within the club between the formal decision-making process and the informal process used to realize ideas and plans. Not everyone appreciates this informality, especially those who learn about the plan by reading the newspaper. A board member admits that "the need to do something was very great but the speed with which this all happened is probably too fast for some"(Anthonissen & Boessenkool, 1998, p. 75).

The plan for setting up the Business club and for obtaining sponsors is publicly announced by board members before the general membership and the multi-club council have even seen the plans. According to several board members this was necessary because the contract with the main sponsor was ending.

The need to sustain the enthusiasm of the new sponsor is the main reason given for the speed in carrying out the plan and not discussing it with the general membership. "We had no choice" says a board member (Anthonissen & Boessenkool, 1998, p. 75). Thus, the decision is justified by appealing to market forces and the best interest of the club. This is simultaneously an appeal to unity and loyalty.

The sudden creation of a foundation leads to confusion among members about the organizational structure of the club. Who is responsible for making and implementing policy? For planning skill development? For the financial aspects of the club? What is the relationship between the board of the football club and that of the foundation? What is the influence of the sponsor? The creation of the Business club means that membership and sponsorship become intertwined. For example, a board member explains that "the main sponsor of PTP is considering the possibility of having someone from their organization become part of the PTP board; we think that is a good idea because it means that he thinks through matters with us" (Anthonissen & Boessenkool, 1998, p. 76). Koski and Heikkala (1997) call this type of overlap mixed rationales. Mixed rationales occur when volunteer members of a club have to work together with professionals who are nonmembers but want to influence the decisions made by the club. The results are not always positive however, due to conflicting motivations of volunteers and professionals. In the current study, some club members are shocked that a seat on the board might be given to a sponsor. The PTP football club has never been known for its professional ways of working but for many members it is increasingly becoming too businesslike. Much criticism is ventilated in the bar and locker room. A club member complains that "responsibilities have not been clearly delineated and the first men's team is being separated from the club" (Anthonissen & Boessenkool, 1998, p. 81).

SHRINKING OPPOSITION

Club members however, fail to speak up when they are given the opportunity to formally address the issues. Only 12 members show up for the general membership meeting. This indicates how the club culture has already changed. A member explains his absence at the meeting: "Ah, they made that choice a long time ago and the general membership meeting is only a formality. I do not think my vote and ideas will have any impact" (Anthonissen & Boessenkool, 1998, p. 81). Other members think the same way: "There is little clarity in the way in which things have been handled. The board lacks the courage to be open and straightforward. I think they are afraid of differences of opinion" (Anthonissen & Boessenkool, 1998, p. 81).

Hegemony occurs when there is (implicit) support for an ideology, making it the dominant ideology (Gramsci 1975 cited in van den Brink, 1978, p. 16). The PTP case is a good illustration of how this works. Club members say they understand the need for top accomplishments in relationship to the pyramidal structure. As long they have access to resources that enable them to play at their level, they agree with the changed pyramid discourse as the sense making structuring principle within the club. This is evident at a general membership meeting. The chair, who has been with the club a long time, asks the small number of members present at the general meeting to trust the direction the council wants to go. The members agree without one dissenting vote while in the hallways before the meeting there was much resistance to the idea. The members who attend the membership meeting think it is good that the board is so involved and keeps the club going. These club members do not want to be held responsible for the continuity of the club. Most of the club members do not attend the meeting, however, and/or are silent. They do so because nothing has changed for them. A member says he realizes that "recreation soccer has been paying the bill for a long time already" (Anthonissen, 1997, p. 13). The principle of being part of the decision making process has vanished as the comment of that member illustrates: "let them arrange everything . . . if they go too far, I am gone" (Anthonissen, 1997, p. 14).

The failure of club members to voice their verbal opposition at the membership meeting is evidence for board members that their decision is the correct one. They now incorporate the interest of external stakeholders into their discourse. They argue that the football club has to operate in a professional or businesslike manner to attract a sponsor. Since sponsors want to know what happens with their money, the club must make a long term plan covering several years. The board argues that this move towards a professional approach cannot be avoided. A board member contends that "the decision making process needs to be more structured; in this day and age you cannot do it any other way"(Anthonissen & Boessenkool, 1998, p. 81). PTP's move towards professionalization is framed as inevitable.

The pronouncements and behavior of the board members and club members sustain and reinforce the dominance of the elite pyramidal discourse. Members do not have enough power to challenge the dominant discourse; their alternate discourses are subsumed into the dominant discourse about the nature of the pyramidal structure. Hargreaves and Tomlinson (1992,) write "hegemony is not simply a question of ideological domination but also of processes by which social agents actively and consciously accommodate each other in pursuit of their perceived interests . . . " (p. 211). Interactions among actors are not only influenced by active and intentional behavior but also influenced by passive behavior; together they can be used to defend self interest (Giddens, 1979). This is true in the PTP case as well. PTP members and board members influence each other by intentionally not taking any action.

Although some members see the solution of the board as innovative and of strategic importance for the club, most members think this choice is incongruent with club culture. Consequently, they have little motivation to get involved or to volunteer in the club. They suspect that board members are primarily furthering their own interests. Board members are portrayed as having little interest in the membership as a whole. In turn, board members reproach club members for lack of involvement with the club as is evident in low attendance at general meetings and a lack of volunteerism. This lack of involvement by the membership means that the focus of board members shifts from the membership to the board itself (and the relations with the club council and external stakeholders). Board members use colleagues at other clubs and sponsors who react positively to PTP's plans, as their sounding board. The gap between the ways board members and the membership now assign meanings to the purpose of the club can be described as estranged (Anthonissen & Boessenkool, 1998). This alienation results in an undemocratic manner of making decisions and an increasingly hierarchical and inequitable structure. This is in sharp contrast to the original organizational form based on democracy and on an interdependent structure and that assumed equal treatment of teams. This change means that club culture is in a state of flux.

CURBING DISSENSION

The board attempts to curb dissension by incorporating the sport for all discourse into the dominant discourse. It tries to reduce the tension by separating the different sources of income and expenditures. They argue that they do not want the other teams to get the feeling that their membership contributions are paying the travel costs of the elite teams. A board member explains that this separation "can work for the benefit of members of the lower teams; otherwise their membership fee would be increased" (Anthonissen & Boessenkool 1998, p. 76).

Club members are less concerned about separate budgets, however, than they are about the rationale for the shift in emphasis and in the interest the board has in the rest of the teams. Athletes wonder if they will receive any attention at all, which they define as being heard and seen by board members and with having access to adequate resources. An athlete who plays on one of the men's senior teams complains that "the last time we played, we used a ball that I suspect they had received as a freebie when they bought a pound of butter" (Anthonissen 1997, p. 13). In the eyes of many members, the amount of attention the board pays to recreational sport, girls' and indoor football is rapidly decreasing. Recreational sport is not even mentioned in the new long-term plan. Athletes who play for the lower division teams acknowledge that better performances by the elite teams are necessary to rebuild and sustain the pyramidal structure but they also want recognition and attention for their own achievements.

This process shows how board members shape their arguments and methods of persuasion to gradually shift to a new discourse. The board increasingly begins to make decisions without asking the general membership. As a result, the club culture that was based on cohesion based on a pyramid structure in which elite and grass root sports are in balance with each other, is changing. The resulting struggle shows that processes of differentiation are occurring although board members still appeal to unity. The ideology that created elite and amateur sport as interdependent and that enhanced organizational unity over the past years, now interferes with the desired unity.

This means that the board can no longer present arguments based on shared norms and values. Similarly, those members who present an alternate viewpoint can no longer base their appeal on a culture that is based on the interdependence of elite and grass roots sport. A few try to think beyond the frame of an interdependent pyramid in order to understand the discourse used by the board. A board member sums up the situation: "It should always be possible for a few teams to play at the elite level; it may not however, occur at the expense of other teams. They should be able to play football in a relaxed and pleasant context" (Anthonissen & Boessenkool, 1998; p. 76). By changing its discourse to legitimate its preference for elite sport, the board has little room for alternate frames, however. This shift has consequences for the board as well however, since it has transferred some of its power of and responsibility for decision making to the Business club.

These developments are not unique to the football club PTP, but occur in many football clubs (Anthonissen & Boessenkool, 1998). Board members of most of the clubs continue to use a discourse that seemingly supports the interdependent relationship between a high level of achievement (elite) and recreational sport (the base) and use it to justify a shift in attention to elite sport. The board of PTP tries to increase the number of members who play at the grass root level by recruiting and paying elite performers from outside the club to come to play for PTP instead of developing and choosing good players from the base of PTP. The members disagree with this strategy; yet the board's intention to develop a broader base (and therefore to restore the pyramid) can be seen as a strategy to sell the idea of an elite team to the members and change the organizational culture.

DEALING WITH DIVERSITY

Organizational culture pertains not only to visible characteristics such as symbols and codes for behavior but also to underlying assumptions (Knoppers & Anthonissen, 2001; Verweel & Knoppers, Chapter 1). These are shared, often subconsciously, by many members of organizations, groups or clubs. If members share underlying assumptions then a basic level of cohesion may be created. Athletes do not become members of a certain club because they like the club colors or the way the bar has been decorated. Such external characteristics may sometimes have a strong symbolic value but only matter when underlying assumptions are challenged (see also Boessenkool, Chapter 4).

PTP board members who want to strengthen unity in the club continually stress that a key assumption of the club is that top-level teams should be embedded in a broad membership base. They try to stimulate the feeling of belonging among members by emphasizing that this underlying assumption is part of the essence of the club. This emphasis on being one big family shows how accentuating the efficacy of cohesion may blind individuals to existing differentiation.

Board members pay little attention to subgroups, subcultures and/or individual differences that exist in the club. This is ironic since many subcultures play a role in PTP such as elite teams, competitive teams, recreational teams, youth teams, a girls' team, indoor football, young people who do not want to play on Saturday, etc. In addition, board members who talk in terms of 'we / they', openly show their preference for a specific group or team and/or focus only on the interests of that group when making decisions. At the same time, different groups and individuals try, if not always actively, to continually promulgate their definition of reality.

Board members continually emphasize the need for unity while they shift the dominant discourse of the club. In other words, they use the integration perspective and in doing so, limit the influence of alternate discourses. Board members emphasize shared values and norms and one membership fee to strengthen unity. A board member argues that: "we are one club. All the adult members pay the same fees. If we create differences in the cost of membership then we will see differences between poor and rich members; we do not want that"(Anthonissen 1997, p. 14).

According to a board member, " the choice for elite football helps those who play in lower division teams; if we did not do this, then membership fees would have to be increased" (Anthonissen & Boessenkool, 1998, p. 76). He emphasizes the benefits the new emphasis has for the lesser skilled athletes in order to justify his own preference for elite football. As a result of this emphasis on unity, disagreements and differences in meanings are discounted since they may negatively reflect on the interests of the dominant [white male] group. In this way, the integration perspective, that is, the emphasis on unity, has also become part of the dominant discourse about the elite pyramidal structure. This emphasis on solidarity and cohesion is also sustained by the importance assigned to social cohesion by others outside the club. National sport associations and governmental officials often point to the potential of sport to strengthen societal cohesion (Elling, De Knop & Knoppers, 2001). References to images of unity and solidarity in the current case study suggest and (re) produce assumptions about the cohesive potential of sport as well.

The idea that consensus, unity and harmony are necessary for organizational productivity and effectiveness, stems from an integration perspective on culture and from a systems approach to thinking about organizations (Martin, 2002; Mastenbroek, 2002; Verweel, 2001; Verweel & Knoppers, Chapter 1).

The discourse employed by PTP to describe the pyramid structure is embedded in an integration perspective and is used to legitimate actions that supposedly promote unity within the club. Board members protect the pyramidal frame while at the same time changing the discursive practices that are associated with it. If there are differences in meaning and the club does not become unified by it self then that unity will be forced upon it. An emphasis on consensus and harmony is used to safeguard the idea of the interdependent pyramid. According to the board, members who are not concerned about unity or harmony challenge the basic assumption that a pyramid provides the best structure.

DISCUSSION AND CONCLUSION

The basic assumption that underlies the thinking of PTP about a pyramidal structure, can best be understood in ideological terms. Convictions are at the center of ideologies and directly and indirectly related to the interests that groups or individuals have. What people perceive as social reality is directly related to the sharing of power at the societal level (macro), within organizations (meso), and within the daily life of individuals (micro). The ideological is therefore "the capability of dominant groups or classes to make their own sectional interests appear to others as universal ones" (Giddens, 1979, p. 6).

This is what board and council members are trying to do at PTP. They transform the meanings they give to a pyramidal structure into a dominant discourse that is situated in an ideology in which elite performance is assumed to take place under equitable conditions (Knoppers & Anthonissen, 2001).

The use of this discourse may give the club an opportunity to create a seemingly unified front and is a temporary but stubborn coagulation of constructions about which there is a great deal of consensus. The focus on consent means also that board members are able to safeguard their own interests and increase their power. By incorporating alternate discourses about self-defined achievement and about solidarity into the dominant discourse, they ensure that their decisions will be supported by at least some of the members. Most club members safeguard their own interests as well. As long as they see enough opportunities to participate in sport at their own level, they will accept the reasoning of the board members. When club members sense that there is little opportunity for them to participate in sport in the ways they would like they leave however, and join another club.

The dominant meanings given to elite sport by board members are also related to societal meanings associated with various forms of sport masculinities (Connell, 1995; Kerfoots & Knight, 1998; Knoppers & Anthonissen, 2001; in press).

In other words, the discourse used by PTP board and council members to legitimate the implementation of an elite pyramidal structure is also a discourse associated with white masculinities. According to Connell (1995) and Whitehead & Barrett (2001), a characteristic of most masculinities is that they differentiate themselves from other masculinities. This is also the case in PTP. The entire process of change in this football club creates and reproduces dominant, complicit, and marginalized masculinities (Connell 1995). The board can be seen as group of white men who create and practice a masculinity that dominates the club, that attempts to win consent for their viewpoints, and that allies itself with men's elite sport.

These board members use the power associated with their position and with meanings that tends to be assigned to men in football, to change the dominant discourse. Concurrently, the reactions of members of the current elite men's team reveal processes of fragmentation. These athletes assign different meanings to the professionalization pyramid than do the board members. Some of the members who play in grass roots teams practice a complicit masculinity by supporting the board's decisions although it may not always be in their best interest. Those men who have constructed alternate discourses and realize that those discourses are marginalized warn they will leave the club if their opportunities to play are affected.

The involvement of board members in this male dominated sport club and their alliance with the elite men's team may mean that board members need not spend much time and effort differentiating themselves from femininities.

They do however differentiate themselves from club members who do not agree with the board's discourse. Meanings assigned by the predominantly white male membership are welcome as long as they concur or reinforce the discourse used by the board.

The club as a whole however, pays a price for the struggles within the board and for the ways in which various masculinities are created and work to differentiate themselves from each other and relate to the shift in discourse. Club members have to cope with a change from a culture that was based on consensus to one that exhibits differentiation and fragmentation.

The emerging culture that accompanies the path to success incorporates a change in meanings given to solidarity and to equality. The definition of equality is framed in terms of a uniform membership fee membership instead of in equal opportunities and resources to play football. The differences in resources and opportunities mean that there is more room for certain forms of masculinity and less for others. The shift in discourse from sport for all to a discourse of professionalism not only stimulates diversity in viewpoints but also illustrates how struggles within the board and between the board and the club members give meanings to social diversity.

Notes
[1] The Football board consists of white men, who are on the average 45 years old, who have been involved with the club for a long time, and, have been members of the lower division teams. The chair comes from a family that has along tradition of charing the football board and the council.
[2] The Dutch Olympic Committee however, encourages clubs to increase and broaden their programs for recreational and lower division athletes.

CHAPTER 4
"IT IS A PROCESS FILLED WITH STRUGGLES":
MERGERS OF SPORT CLUBS

Jan Boessenkool

"Giving up the name [of a club] is like dying a little; someone who just trades away the name and date of incorporation, does not care about the club". (athlete)

"If you do not accept our proposals and decisions, then we resign." (Club chair)

OVERVIEW

Prior to 1990 Dutch amateur sport clubs were involved in about thirty mergers. Since 1990 there have been more than a hundred mergers and many ongoing discussions about possible mergers. Explanations for this trend have included the assumption that a small club cannot survive because a bigger club is a better and more visible club, the pressure placed on sport clubs by national sport associations and local governments, the increase in governmental and sport regulations, and, a decrease in the financial resources of sport clubs. Processes of the merger of football clubs tend to receive little scholarly attention as processes of sense making. In this chapter, I describe and analyze the assignment of meanings during the merger process involving two football clubs, Bunder and Donaro. I explore how various actors negotiate the sense making process so that certain meanings become dominant and decisive for the direction and outcome of the merger process. At first glance, amateur sport clubs seem to be quite similar to each other. During processes of merger, however, many differences become visible and important to members, ranging from identity questions to topics like the level of play, club colors, and, the exact date of the beginning of the new club. The merger process becomes a complicated development in which members sometimes concur, occasionally disagree completely, and, now and then form unexpected coalitions within and across two merging clubs.

RESEARCH QUESTION AND METHODOLOGY:

To what extent are processes that occur during the merger of two football clubs layered and which power struggles occur in the decision making process in the creation of the new club?

The data are drawn from a qualitative research project that explored the mergers of twenty amateur football clubs in the Netherlands between 1994 and 1998 (Anthonissen & Boessenkool, 1998). The researchers analyzed relevant documents such as newspaper articles and minutes of meetings, interviewed hundred and twenty board members, athletes and other club members and stakeholders, and, observed approximately thirty committee and general membership meetings. All of the sport administrators and officials directly involved in the various mergers are white and almost all are male. In this case study I present the merger process of merging using the data from the merger of two clubs, Donaro and Bunder, as an example. The introduction to Chapter 1 has already given a snapshot of part of that process. In the discussion I will also refer to other mergers that have been part of the research project.

MOVING TOWARDS A MERGER

Bunder was begun in 1908 as a secular amateur football club. Currently it sponsors 25 teams and has about 500 members, including 300 youth. Its top men's team has always played at a relative high level; much of the involvement of the club's members is in service of this team.

Relatively little attention is paid to those who play in lower divisions and to the youth teams. During the past several years, the number of youth and senior members has begun to decrease and the shortage of coaches, team leaders, committee members and board members has become acute. The budget has also become a concern since the board members of the club want to see its first men's team play in a higher division, which requires an expensive coach. In addition, sponsors who invest a lot in the club want results and a say in decisions about the club. In other words, Bunder is in a state of flux.

Donaro was started in 1951 as a Roman Catholic football club. The membership list is filled with people with the same last name because it is a family club. The club sponsors 12 teams and has about 300 members, including 150 youth. Although the top men's team plays in the lowest division of the national football association (KNVB), the club has always made ends meet. The former chair of the board of directors says: "If we needed money, we held a flea market that was always a success" (Anthonissen & Boessenkool, 1998, p. 170). A pleasant and cozy social climate is valued more than a first team that plays at the elite level.

The men's first team likes to win but the club is not prepared to pay exorbitant amounts for a coach. The number of (youth) members who play football is decreasing, perhaps because Donaro is situated in a relative wealthy village. A member explains: "It is of course a village with standing; football does not have a high priority with us" (Anthonissen & Boessenkool, 1998, p. 171). There is rarely a shortage of coaches and volunteers although it is these individuals who are having second thoughts about the merger between the two clubs from the same village. When rumors about a merger emerge, Donaro's members fear that their club will be swallowed up by and disappear into the larger Bunder club.

There is no pressing need for the two clubs to merge but the officials of both clubs have noticed merger mania elsewhere. The minutes of 12 December 1990 of one of the clubs reads: "Close cooperation between the two clubs resulting in a merger, is the only way to keep football at an acceptable level; this is also necessary to keep the youth" (Anthonissen & Boessenkool, 1998, p. 171). Such comments set the tone and the exploration period begins. The first talks accomplish little. The successive attempts are usually couched in discussions concerning finances and the sport itself. The discussions are unsuccessful due to disagreement about a new name, the rehashing of old feelings and discussions dating to 1972, and, the seemingly mounting differences in mentality. When the assumption of equality between the two clubs is called into question, the independence of the clubs is emphasized. A Donaro board member explains that "we are a healthy club and can stand on our own feet" (Anthonissen & Boessenkool, 1998, p. 228).

The village square becomes a place where all these matters are discussed since everyone in the village knows each other. The local media urge the village council to decrease its financial support of the clubs if they refuse to merge. A sport journalist writes " . . . a merger of the two clubs has financial and organizational advantages and guarantees a more efficient use of facilities." (Local paper, 09-10-1992). The local government puts the clubs under pressure to merge by threatening with privatization; a city official implies that funds will be more readily available if the merger goes through (Local paper, 09-10-1992).

Although little is accomplished in the following years, discussions to actualize the merger are begun in 1995. Differences in opinion about various matters are recognized but the emphasis in the discussions is on financial matters. Some people expect that the merger will result in financial efficiency. There are other secondary arguments cited in favor of the merger. A large club is assumed to draw more youth, to result in a higher level of performance of the men's first team, to attract more and better qualified coaches, to lower membership fees, to strengthen feelings of loyalty toward the club, to increase the income from sponsors, to permit the building of an indoor training facility and bleachers for the spectators, and, to result in more clout in negotiations with the local government.

Members of the boards of directors of both clubs participate in the first formal meeting about the merger; they appoint a merger committee with as chair someone who is not associated with either of the two clubs and is well respected in the village.

The chairs of both clubs expect that there will be several hassles about name and club colors of the new club but emphasize that all decisions concerning the merger should/will be based on rational and businesslike arguments and not on emotional grounds (minutes, 17-01-1995). In this way they attempt to rule out emotional arguments ahead of time and try to emphasize the importance of reaching consensus.

The process leading toward the merger is filled with power struggles that are characterized by distrust despite good intentions and positive attitudes of those involved. The chair of the merger committee seems to recognize the potential pitfalls from the outset. At the first meeting of the committee, he proclaims that "the fans, members and people outside the clubs will try to drive a wedge between the two clubs.

We can only reach the finish line by using persuasion and forming a block" (Anthonissen & Boessenkool, 1998, p. 234). Although he seems to realize that differentiation and fragmentation will occur, the chair of the merger committee stresses that the merger can become a success only when board members use an integration perspective.

DISTRUST AND POWER STRUGGLES

DIFFERENCES IN SENSE MAKING AMONG BOARD MEMBERS

Distrust and power struggles emerge almost immediately. The struggles are initially confined to the merger committee meetings with the chairs of the two clubs as key participants. They fight at almost every meeting about issues such as errors in the minutes, communication with the media, the club members and with the sponsors, the type of club uniforms, and, the content of the bylaws. Rational arguments and an emphasis on the importance of consensus are usually used to end the discussion but the hatchet is never actually buried. Other committee members either choose sides or keep their distance.

Most of the power in the clubs lies with the board members since they are much better informed than other club members. There is little evidence at the outset of a power struggle between board and club members and about perceived inequalities in power between the two clubs. Yet different factors determine the degree of power that is brought to the bargaining table such as geography (where members live), the importance assigned to religion and religious practices, the culture of each club, types of sponsors, and, the degree of emphasis on elite competition for the first men's team.

The chair of Donaro, a club with Roman Catholic roots, for example, continually stresses equality and club identity while the chair of Bunder, a club with a high-level performance orientation, emphasizes the sport-related advantages of the merger. These differences in values continually underlie the discussions about integration, unity and consensus during the negotiations but they are not recognized and not accepted as part of historical and logical differences. They are not allowed to make a difference. In other words, possibilities for diversity of meanings are circumscribed.

The chair of Donaro is one of the merger committee members but he resigns after a half year. He says his resignation has nothing to do with personality differences but with the actions of the Bunder chair. The Donaro chair attributes his resignation to the delaying tactics of the Bunder chair who, according to him, keeps revisiting the duly recorded decisions. He accuses the Bunder chair of contributing little to the merger and of leaking confidential memos to the press. The vice chair of Donaro replaces him in the merger committee.

Despite the resignation and existing differences, the clubs continue on the path toward the merger and battles continue to rage. Stopping the merger process is defined as "failure" (interview records; minutes of meetings, 1995). Obviously there is little acceptance of existing differences in sense making.

The mistrust between the two clubs, and especially between members of both boards, is also revealed in the resistance of the two clubs to share their financial documents. This refusal/inability continues to erode the assumption of equal partnership with which the process was begun and continues even when the merger is formally completed. Minutes of meetings and interviews reveal questions such as: "How large are the contributions of the sponsors?" "What is the value of the buildings and of the mortgage?" Both clubs have a sponsor. One of the chairs works for the club's sponsor. "Who will be the chief sponsor now?" "How will the ideas of sponsors influence the merger?" These are questions that are of little concern to athletes and other club members but are important to board members.

The differences among board members feed the underlying mistrust and the assumption of hidden agendas. Consequently, the negotiations in creating a new club are given a zero sum character and do not construct the merger as a mutually beneficial situation. This zero sum approach is created back stage but comes to the forefront during general meetings and occasionally in newspaper articles. This approach manifests itself in the nominations for board members of the new club. Will a chair be someone not affiliated with either club? Will every position such as treasurer, chair and secretary be shared? The latter option may be a short-term solution but in the end it favors one club more than the other. The actual winners and losers are only evident several years later.

DIFFERENCES IN SENSE MAKING BETWEEN CLUB AND BOARD MEMBERS

The process in choosing the new club's name reveals the distrust and power struggles that have characterized the negotiations/talks. Athletes and other club members are invited to submit ideas for a new name in writing. A committee, consisting of individuals who are not associated with either club, is appointed to recommend a new name. The Name Committee consists of the village mayor, a well-known former football player, and, an advertising expert. The merger committee decides that the recommendation of the Name Committee will be binding. After much deliberation, the Name Committee recommends *Synergus* as a suitable name. For more than a year, club members have left most of the negotiations up to the governing boards of the clubs. Now they become upset when they are confronted with the results. They express their anger in newspaper articles and in discussions in the village square. A board member sighs: "One should never involve members in decisions about the details of a merger. They can have a voice and submit ideas but they should not expect that their opinions will always be honored" (Anthonissen & Boessenkool, 1998, p. 183). Another board member thinks that it is better for the club board members to decide the new name and club colors before the merger and then "announce the decision to the members" (Anthonissen & Boessenkool, 1998, p. 186). At the same time, board members fight among themselves about every possible issue. Ironically, board members have a difficult time forging consensus among the different and fragmented meanings assigned to the merger by club members while at the same time there is little agreement within the merger committee and governing boards.

Matters seem to come to a head. At the annual membership meeting of Bunder, 68 of the 69 present vote against the new name. The Donaro board warns its members that it will resign if the name is not accepted. Letters to the editor appear in the local newspaper. One letter writer complains that "the choice for the name Synergus reveals a total lack of fantasy" and argues "for a real Dutch name" (Anthonissen & Boessenkool, 1998, p. 186). Eventually members accept the new name but do so only because the boards of both clubs had committed themselves to the choice of the Name Committee in advance. The choice is limited to either accepting the new name or ending the whole merger process. The board therefore uses its position of power to force consensus on the name issue. This procedure and its results however, seem to add oil to the merger fire.

COMPLETING THE MERGER

There are other unforeseen complications. Discussions of the merger committee with village representatives lead to more confusion because it is not clear what is agreed upon (minutes of meetings of merger committee, 1996).

One assumption underlying the beginnings of the merger process had been that the newly formed club would receive a substantial subsidy from the local government. This turns out not to be true. Also, a sponsor succeeds in being appointed to the board of the newly created club although there are board and club members who do not want him there.

Legal aspects cloud the merger even more. It is not clear what is legally required, what the difference is between a legal and practical merger, what the bylaws and club rules should contain, what the role of the national soccer association (KNVB) should be, and, where advice about these matters can be obtained. In other words, there is much confusion and mutual distrust. The merger, however, is assumed to be unavoidable. It is increasingly seen as the solution to many problems, including finances and performance of the future men's first team. Board members have moved cultural differences between the clubs and emotional aspects such as loss of identity, to the background.

After the merger is complete in 1996, the former chair of Bunder says that the merger was about emotions and that nothing was gained from it. He regrets the merger, "not because of the members but because it was an organizational disaster involving board members, the national soccer association and the local government." His rival, the former chair of Donaro, agrees and also cites the power struggle: "Bunder dominated everything after the merger" (Anthonissen & Boessenkool 1998, p. 202).

This merger has other effects as well. Many trained volunteers have left the club. Several of them remark that "we do not come anymore because we do not feel at home" (Anthonissen & Boessenkool 1998, p. 203).

There are few gains and many losses. The number of members of Synergus is less than half of that what the combined two clubs had before the merger. Those who left have stopped playing football or have joined another club. Instead of moving to a higher division, the men's first team has dropped to a lower level. In summary, the merger did not have the expected results.

Obviously the creation of Synergus was accompanied by struggles on many fronts. It is primarily the board members who control the struggle in the merger arena, in the assignment of meanings to various events, and, in visions and projections for the future. The daily struggle for dominance in the assignment of meanings is a struggle for power.

THE SPORT CLUB AS AN ARENA

Before the merger, Donaro and Bunder were independent social systems each with its own historically determined structure and symbols. Slowly but surely its actors, especially board members and some of the trained volunteers, want to align their club with developments outside the clubs. In addition, the shortage of volunteers, complex rules and regulations, and, inadequate financing are reason enough to act. The disappointment in the performance of the men's first team of Bunder also plays a role. Consequently, the clubs leave a relatively peaceful arena and enter the turbulent arena of mergers. Struggles occur in this arena that are related to struggles within each club and to inter-club differences. Each confrontation reveals meanings assigned to a hidden part of the previous system that board members had not taken into account. The struggle continually involves sense making and the subsequent question: Whose meanings will dominate and result in action? Although the creation of Synergus as a club is unique, the process of its creation involves several patterns that are common to merger processes.

EXERCISING POWER

The sense making of board members tends to dominate the process of mergers, including that which created Synergus. When board members interact with club members, they tend to use a dominant discourse that emphasizes a pyramidal structure and that constructs the club as a unified whole (see also Anthonissen, Chapter 3). Yet cultural differences, power and emotions are the cornerstones in the construction/creation of clubs like Synergus although board members vary in the ways in which they use and name them however. Mergers tend to begin with an emphasis on rational objectives that gradually disappear into the background (Koot & Hogema, 1992).

The topics of the struggles change regularly but the past, positions, perspectives, meanings, and vested interests of the most important actors and the nature of the relationships with other actors, barely change during the merger process. These are continually reproduced and are characteristic of a merger process (Coenen, 1989). A few of the actors fall by the way side. Most of the struggles among board members usually occur back stage, out of sight of club members. The latter learn about the struggles primarily through the press or in other informal ways. In other words, their ways of making sense of the situation are influenced by the press and other actors.

Power is both relative and relational however. All members have power but some use it more than others. Athletes for example, can exercise their power in a general membership meeting and/or by leaving the club, which some of them actually do. Obviously however, the struggle between board members and athletes and other club members is unequal. Board members often determine the direction of the club. Club members give themselves very little power in the membership meeting although formally they have the final say. The acquiescence of the athletes and other club members stems in part from a fear that the board may resign. Club members do not want to be without a board or become board members. Ironically, the struggle among board members themselves is also a power struggle. Coalitions continually change and strong-minded individuals try to guide the process in the direction they want it to go. Groups that seemed to be homogeneous at the start of the merger process turn out to be heterogeneous and fragmented.

The actors in the struggle have various weapons. Some enjoy the support of a large group, some have a strong personality, and, others have considerable knowledge about the situation and/or mergers. As Verweel (Chapter 2) points out, sport organizations, just like other organizations, are half-open systems with flexible boundaries. Processes within an organization are directly related to those outside it. Board members base their actions on their interactions with athletes and other club members and with actors outside the clubs (stakeholders) such as the village council, the media and the national football association (KNVB). Although stakeholders initially have relative little influence, actors assign different meanings to this influence.

INFLUENCE OF STAKEHOLDERS

Local government

The local government is an important stakeholder in more than the half of the merger processes studied (Anthonissen & Boessenkool, 1998). Often its sport and recreational division initiates the idea of a merger by creating a policy intended to reduce the number of football clubs and thus save money. When the village or town budget needs to be reduced, sport related items are the first to be eliminated. Grants and subsidies are reduced and the rent for use of the football fields is increased. In addition, real estate developers are often interested in the land on which a sport club stands. These factors lead to discussions between local government officials and board members. Differences in meanings emerge in those discussions, including those involving the merger of Donaro and Bunder. Local city councils often prefer to have a large multi- sport club at the edge of town and to sell the rest of the land. Board members suspect that local governments increase the rent to force clubs to embrace a merger and that the city sees primarily the financial side and ignores the sport-related or social aspects of the merger.

The struggle between local government officials and board members usually does not polarize the two parties. Instead, board members assign their own meanings to the discussions and situate them in their thinking about the future of the club. They construct themselves as the victims of external developments and pressure from stakeholders such as the local government. Simultaneously they use this pressure as an excuse or opportunity to develop a more commercial and professional club. This is the reason why many clubs initially cooperate with the local government and hold high expectations for this cooperative venture. This enthusiasm wanes when it becomes clear that the local government's primary aim is to cut the budget, not to increase subsidies.

The high expectations that board members have for the involvement of the local government are replaced by disappointment and an increasing sense that the local government is more an opponent than a partner. Powerlessness and anger then shape the relationship. Board members gradually discover that local governing councils say much but do little. A few boards of directors realize this early in the merger process and try to milk the situation for all it is worth. If for example, the sport fields have become part of the plans for a new housing development, the sport club uses all sorts of legal procedures to delay these plans until the local council gives them certain concessions.

The press

The press also becomes an important stakeholder in various ways during a merger. When the first merger attempt of Donaro and Bunder fails, the press accuses the clubs of wanting to hold on to their uniqueness and the status quo. Editorials argue that the uniqueness of the clubs is outdated, that a merger has financial and organizational advantages, and, that it is time for the local government to interfere by forcing the clubs to merge. In addition the press contends that it is a misuse of tax funds to give separate grants to each club if the clubs can function more efficiently and save money by merging. Such press coverage works to the advantage of board members who favor a merger. It encourages them to argue that they also want to let go of the past and to make a new start based on an assumption of equality between the two clubs and with the use of a business like approach. They are aware of differences between the two clubs but describe them as differences in mentality that should not play a prominent role in the process.

Obviously then, the meanings created by stake holders can greatly influence processes of sense making within sport clubs and can sometimes play a decisive role. Still, pressure from stakeholders does not create a united front. Much work must be done within the club to get athletes to support proposed changes.

Layers in the Arena

Not only the context but also the arena is layered, consisting of a front stage, back stage and under the stage (Bailey, 1977). A decade ago the general membership meeting (front stage) was the most important and powerful place for making policy decisions about a sport club. Most of the members or athletes knew enough about the club to make informed decisions. Outside influences on club life were rare. Board members spent more time on tasks such as controlling expenditures, preparing for members' meetings and party evenings and organizing teams, than on shaping and making strategic decisions for the club. This has changed however. The front stage no longer shapes decisions but only takes decisions. The more formal part of the decision making process takes place in board and committee meetings while a large part is pushed to back stage and under the stage and is no longer visible.

Merger committees tend to operate back stage. The club board appoints the members of these committees (as they do other ad hoc committees). In other words, the general membership meeting has little say about the beginning of a merger process. Sometimes the general membership meeting gives a merger committee a mandate to explore merger possibilities but usually contacts have already been made with possible merger partners before the general membership is formally involved. The football world is relatively small and many people know each other. The nature of these contacts determines to a large degree the success of the merger talks. If board members, especially chairs, can get along well with each other then the merger can be completed in a few months. They work back stage and often under the stage to be able to present the merger plan front stage in a general membership meeting. The athletes and other members, who have barely noticed that these discussions have been taking place, can only say yes or no. A governing board may even threaten to resign if athletes vote against a merger.

In cases where merger negotiations do not go well back stage and/or under the stage, as was the case with Synergus, the chairs seek support among their members in various ways. They use general membership meetings and interviews with the media to create support for their viewpoints. The fights for seats in the new board of Synergus occur back and under the stage.

The members of the merger committee are well versed in the necessary information while other board members are happy if they are kept up to date. Decisions about mergers are made primarily by the boards of the clubs and usually only by a few people. A board member says: "In order to realize a merger, you have to get four or five people together who trust each other and work well together, and then you will get the rest of the board members behind you" (Anthonissen & Boessenkool 1998, p. 222).

Although it is the athletes and other club members who ultimately decide at the general meeting, their choices are limited. Board members rarely consult athletes and other club members and often work independently of, or around, their opinions and ideas. General membership meetings are poorly attended unless the merger is discussed. Possibly this increase in attendance in conjunction with a merger occurs because members are afraid of being taken over by another club, of losing their position on a team or as volunteer, and/or of losing club identity. Board members then have to convince the members that a merger is the only rational way to go and that they, as board, will do everything possible to hold on to that that is unique to the club. In this way the club board uses the front stage to legitimate their back stage and under the stage behavior.

THE POWER OF IDENTITY AND SYMBOLS

Individuals want to be part of something and at the same time differentiate themselves from others (Verweel, Chapter 2). Music, drama, politics and sport clubs serve to meet a need for identification and social ties. Such ties become more pronounced during negotiation processes involving mergers. The strength of these ties can block or even stop mergers. The resistance to mergers indicates that the symbolic power of membership can transcend the financial and rational reasons that start the merger process. Although the last decade has seen an increase in the diversity of meanings that members of a sport club assign to their club membership, members do not want to give up the familiar during a merger. This is evidenced by the high attendance at membership meetings when mergers are discussed and especially, when the name of the new club is on the agenda.

The struggle for a new name reveals the social-cultural values assigned to club membership. Most board members tend to attach relatively little importance to the topics of name, date of incorporation and club colors. They are topics that can stop the merger process however; "some mergers are not completed because athletes do not want or like the proposed changes." (Anthonissen & Boessenkool, 1998, p. 186). Changing the name of a club is an emotional experience because it often means letting go off the past and/or it suggests the past is unimportant. A club member says: "Giving up the name is like dying a little; someone who just trades away the name and date of incorporation, does not care about the club" (Anthonissen & Boessenkool, 1998, p. 226). The name is a symbol for all the members but especially for those who have been members for twenty to thirty years.

Some members of Donaro and Bunder argue that a totally new name should be selected for the newly created club because a name that is a combination of the two names is always an expression of inequality. A member contends that "you have to forget the differences and continue as one club" (Anthonissen & Boessenkool 1998, p. 225). This argument reflects a wish to start anew as a whole and to create a new culture. Members of merging clubs, however, often want a name in which they can recognize the old club. A combination name allows this and keeps the past alive. Some see combination names as a reflection of a take over. The first named is the dominant party and takes over the club that has the second name; after a period of time, many members of the secondly named club have left because they do not recognize their original club in the merger club (Anthonissen & Boessenkool, 1998). They do not identify with the new club. They lose their tie with it and search for something else where they will feel they belong.

In general, the value assigned to cultural aspects of membership in a sport club is underestimated in mergers (Anthonissen & Boessenkool, 1998). Club membership obviously means more than training in an adequate facility, having sponsors for shirts, and playing at a high or low competitive level. The diversity of meanings given to membership emerges when club leaders emphasize objectivity and instrumentality arguing that sport clubs require a businesslike and professional approach (see also Anthonissen, Chapter 3). This assessment may be realistic but it is questionable if this reflects the various perceptions of the members themselves. A merger or a more businesslike approach may be necessary for survival but sport clubs are also cultural phenomena. Members see a merger as a necessary evil for survival instead of as a challenge for the future. Being an athlete means more than just throwing or kicking a ball. Board members often tend to misjudge the cultural-emotional meanings assigned to club membership. Of course, they themselves experience such cultural losses in mergers as well since they are also members of the club.

BOARD MEMBERS AS CENTRAL ACTORS

Board members begin a merger process with good intentions and with rational arguments based on the assumption that this will have positive consequences for the club. At that time they see their efforts as a way to keep the sport for all/interdependent pyramid structure intact (Anthonissen, Chapter 3). If they succeed in strengthening the pyramid, then their status as leaders will also increase. When it looks like they might lose the power struggle, they use more emotional topics such as the selection of a name and the incorporation date, to mobilize support for the chosen direction. Slowly the original intentions fade into the background as board members become involved in such struggles. Consequently, both board members and athletes are important actors in the arena of mergers.

The desire of board members to operate a sport club in a more efficient, professional and businesslike manner is not unique to the sport setting but reflects overall societal trends. The merger process, with its accompanying call for unity and consensus, is the board's answer to the question of increasing diversity in meanings assigned to club membership and sport among the members, and, of increasingly fragmented influences from society in general. Board members try to achieve their objective of having the men's first team participate and win in top-level competition by emphasizing the need for unity and the fact that everyone/the club will benefit from this change.

The merger process between two or more clubs begins however with an assumption of diversity, that is, that the two clubs are both similar and dissimilar and offer each other something that the other does not have. Board members dream of large and healthy clubs in which the men's first team competes and wins at the elite level. They discuss this with each other and with colleagues at other clubs and slowly the fire of enthusiasm for a merger and fielding a top-level team is kindled. Most members are unaware of this dynamic because they are more occupied with material aspects such as weekly matches and practices and being together. They only sit up and take notice if these material aspects are affected. By that time, the merger process is underway already. Subsequently, the struggle by board members to strengthen the dominant discourse on the front of the stage intensifies since that discourse will decide much of the nature of the future club.

The differences in mentality that the press and many board members discount in merger processes, play a prominent role at moments in the process when athletes give other meanings to the idea of merging than the board has done and subsequently, challenge the dominant discourse about the merger. The financial and sport advantages may not seem so desirable to them; club members may even assume that each club can continue to operate independently. The struggles about the legitimacy of discourses of board members and of athletes and other club members are not the only ones, however. Board members also struggle with each other about different visions and goals. The actual negotiations involve various struggles front, back and under the stage; each board member strives to emerge as winner in these struggles.

This means that various meanings gradually become congruent with the personal interests and objectives of certain individuals. These individual objectives and interests are not necessarily in opposition to those of the board or club as a whole but they do ensure a struggle will occur. The assignment of meanings and the struggle for dominance or acceptance of a discourse is never smooth especially when there are multiple meanings involved. Yet, eventually the discourse that constructs the merger as having a positive impact on finances and top performance wins and becomes the dominant public discourse. Consequently the new club is the result of a power struggle and its creation reflects a forced unity. Alternate discourses have lost but have not disappeared.

As I said earlier, board members primarily use an economic rationale to decide initiate the idea of a merger. They seek legitimization for it and for the meanings they give to it. They tend to ignore the emotional and cultural meanings given to club membership and to being an athlete. Verweel (2000) points out that when managers or directors use an economic rationale to defend organizational processes, they bring primarily the physical, rational and business side of an organization into focus.

Organizational members, who in this case study are the athletes, agree with the economic rationale until it affects them personally. Everything is acceptable until it affects their practices, competitions, bridge evenings, parties, and so on. This is true for board members as well but they look at it differently. They want a unified club to ensure that the men's first team can compete at the highest possible level; this participation at a high level is assumed to give the club more allure and attract more members. The use of this rationale also assumes that a merger will benefit everyone regardless of the economic changes that accompany a merger.

Board members present the economic approach on front stage but often fail to facilitate the merger process and tend to ignore the ties athletes have with their club, their sport, their team and at what impacts them emotionally. Some board members understand that the merger may mean a loss of identity but see it as a sentimental loss and do not realize and accept differences in sense making. In addition, the resistance to the merger is often not clear- cut and unorganized. Those who resist usually do not have much power either. Only during and at the end of the merger process do board members realize that non-economic forces influence the processes and outcomes of the merger struggle and the arena as a whole. By that time it is often too late.

Verweel (1987) argues that interactions in organizational processes consist of competitive struggles.

> The type of weapons chosen, the cleverness of the parties involved, the prescribed rules and the positions that people take in the arena, result in inequality in power among the participating parties… The arena is not a playground in which the play assumes equality in the beginning and that the game can be started anew each time with the same resources, but it is sometimes a merciless competition in which earlier interactions have already been taken into account in positioning, status in the arena and sometimes even in the structure of the struggle (p. 98).

Board members conduct this struggle on several fronts: with athletes, with the potential merger partner, and with stakeholders. Positions of power differ and everyone has various and different weapons and skills. This does not mean that losers and winners are clear-cut. The struggle can take unexpected turns due to the availability of new resources and the formation of new coalitions. The process has several rules that are open to various interpretations. The strongest have the advantage but they are never completely in charge. Results are often unpredictable.

Despite these inequitable factors, board members frequently use the notion of equality or consensus in sense making in their front stage performance during the merger process.

They insist that there is equality between the organizations in the beginning and that everyone will benefit. Research points out that this is rarely the case (see for example Schenk, 1996; Boessenkool, Van der Spek & Anthonissen, 1997). Most mergers, including those by profit organizations, can best be described afterwards as a take over. The struggle is longest and most intense when initial positions of power are about equal. In the case of Synergus, there are no clear winners, only losers.

CONCLUSION

The results of this research suggest that the influence of perspectives about diversity held by board members, situational specificity, a multi-layered arena, limited predictability, and, struggles for power determine how meanings are assigned in interactions about a merger within sport clubs. This ways in which sense making is continually negotiated in sport clubs in general, and mergers in particular, suggest that sport clubs can be seen as arenas in which the dominance of a specific frame is determined by relations of power that include stakeholders.

The diversity of viewpoints in the arena of mergers is strongly related to positions that board members hold. These positions often are, or become, congruent with individual interests and objectives. These interests and objectives always play an important role in the sense making process and the frames that direct it. Simultaneously, the various interests create room for unexpected coalitions among actors in the arena and with stakeholders. Interactions among all these actors take place only partially on the front stage where board members try to reach consensus in the club in order to proceed in the negotiations with the merger partner.

They want to be backed by their athletes and other club members. The interactions that have the greatest influence on the outcomes of merger processes between amateur sport clubs occur however, back stage and even under the stage. Obviously then, such processes of merger are layered although board members hold onto an integration perspective.

CHAPTER 5
"THE SKILL LEVELS OF MEN ARE QUITE DIVERSE": GENDER AND COACHING

Annelies Knoppers

OVERVIEW

Due to their working relationship with athletes and their visibility, coaches play a crucial role in introducing, reinforcing, and challenging dominant discourses in sport. Their discursive practices impact athletes directly. Such discourses reflect, among other things, how coaches think and talk about social group diversity such as gender, race/ethnicity, age, and sexual preference. Coaches also tend to be the only volunteers in sport clubs who receive remuneration that ranges from coverage of expenses to a specific amount for their work, especially if they are certified and coaching at a high level. In addition, as the description of the Dutch sport system suggests, coaches in the Netherlands are positioned differently from other sport administrators (Verweel & Knoppers, Chapter 1). The use of multi-level coaching certification systems by all sport associations means that coaches are often the only ones working in the club system who are specifically trained for their position. Those who wish to coach elite teams must possess the appropriate certificate offered by a sport association. Such certification systems create an occupational hierarchy. Women coaches are under-represented at all levels in this hierarchy and, as often happens in managerial work, the higher the occupational level, the fewer the number of women coaches.[1] The massive increase in the number of women athletes that began about 30 years ago, has not translated into a similar increase in women in positions of leadership in sport. A change in this dynamic requires strategic policy interventions based on scholarship that exposes ideologies on which discourses are based and reveals areas of resistance and obstacles that keep women out of such positions. Acker (2000), a scholar in the area of gender and organizations, suggests that understanding the ways gender is constructed in a particular situation necessitates an examination of the ideologies are used to legitimate gender inequality. Since ideologies are explicitly expressed in discourses and discursive practices, a study of discourses used by Dutch coaches to explain the skewed gender ratio may give insight into the ways sport and gender ideologies intersect to shape sport in Dutch society.

RESEARCH QUESTION AND METHODOLOGY

What are the dominant themes used by coaches to talk about gender in sport? How might these themes contribute to the skewed gender ratio in coaching?

I base my analysis on data from two studies. One study examines the extent to which men and women coaches in ten sports ((handball, korfball, volleyball, hockey, football, basketball, swimming, tennis, athletics and cycling) give meaning to gender and to the culture in which they coach (Knoppers & Bouman, 1996; 1998). More than 720 coaches completed written questionnaires; eight coaches were interviewed per sport. The other study explored the gendering of images and portrayal of football coaches (Knoppers & Elling, 1999; 2001). This study included interviews with 95 athletes, ten coaches, and, a content analysis of football magazines and coaching materials. In this Chapter I use primarily the data from semi-structured interviews with the 90 coaches that pertain to their discussions of topics related to the skewed gender ratio, to their own experiences as coach, and, to their views on the ways diversity is managed in their club, district and association/federation. These were experienced and certified coaches since on the average they had been coaching for about 11 years and all possessed at least a certificate or a diploma. Men and women comprised 57% and 43% respectively of the coaches who were interviewed. At the time of the interviews, 80% of the women and 50% of the men were coaching women's teams. Four percent of the women and 18% of the men coached men's teams. The other coaches coached mixed gender teams (primarily in korfball, athletics, tennis, swimming).

The research question was used as a guideline in an inductive search of the interview data for emerging constructions of meanings. This search of the data revealed that coaches make sense of the skewed gender ratio by using discourses of 'meritocracy and neutrality', and of 'male dominance and female subordination'. Although these constructions of meanings overlap a great deal with each other, they will be presented separately for clarity. The relationships between both ways of sense making are discussed in the latter part of the chapter.[2]

MAKING SENSE OF MERITOCRACY AND NEUTRALITY

A prevailing strategy these coaches use to explain the skewed gender ratio in coaching are aligned with dominant meanings given to sport performance in organized Dutch sport (Knoppers & Anthonissen, 2001). Most of the coaches see meanings given to performance as objective and neutral since performance is measurable in a quantitative way. In addition, the interviewees tend to place the most value on the performances that are 'faster' and 'better'. They profess not to see the gender of the performer but only the performance itself so that the gender of the best athletes is immaterial to them. The coaches frequently use the argument that if a woman held the record as the world's fastest human being, she would be treated the way elite male athletes are treated. This way of sense making, that frames meanings given to sport performance as neutral and that sees sport as a site of meritocracy, dominates the discussions of the coaches about gendered skewness.

The high value placed on outstanding athletic performance is embedded in definitions and evaluations of coaching. These coaches define a good coach as someone who can demonstrate skills and who can outperform the athletes in these skills. A coach explains: "The best coaches are those guys who have played at the top and can convey that experience to their athletes" (Knoppers & Bouman, 1998, p. 52). In other words, a good coach is someone who is or was an outstanding athlete and/or can outperform her or his athletes. A coach explains that "you have to have played football yourself, perhaps not at the professional level, but you have to be able to keep up physically with the team" (Knoppers & Elling, 1999, p. 12). Another football coach argues that "If you as coach cannot handle a ball in a skillful manner then you will not get respect from the players, even if they are very young" (Knoppers & Elling, 2001, p. 24). A woman coach in athletics explains why she cannot coach elite male athletes:

> If I could run 10 kilometers in 32 minutes I could train group 1 or 2 [men's groups] but I can't keep up with them. Before I am out the door, they are around the corner. I can't run a long distance with them because a coach has to be able to stay with the group. You have to be able to run to the front of the group [to explain things], run with those in the back; you have to run extra (Knoppers & Bouman 1998, p. 127).

Coaches usually retire when they can no longer keep up with their team. A football coach explains: "I think most coaches can coach until they are 50, although it becomes increasingly difficult since you must be in great shape to keep up with the team. Otherwise players lose their respect for you" (Knoppers & Elling, 2001, p. 27).

This performance-based aspect of coaching may explain why most of these coaches range in age between 30 and 40 years and on the average, plan to coach no more than another ten years. The relevance of this performance criterion to coaching expertise is rarely questioned by these coaches. A few coaches however, do not agree with this performance dimension of coaching. A male coach says: "[Your own] technique does not have to be a problem. You let an athlete demonstrate who has the right technique. You only have to be very good in explaining what you want done. You have to be very good in that" (Knoppers & Bouman, 1996, p. 41). Such comments are rare, however. In general there is consensus that coaches have to outperform their athletes and that the standards for becoming a coach do not differentiate between men and women.

The high value placed on coaches being skilled performers is visible in the structure of coaching certification programs. Most certification programs have a skill component that is based on male norms. Specifically, those wanting to enroll in and pass any certification course must pass skills tests to be admitted and succeed in other skill tests to receive the certificate. 'Performing well' in most sport tests means being able to execute skills in the manner of skilled men. A woman coach says: "I don't think I can ever become head coach. You need at least two diplomas for that; it was difficult enough for me as a woman to get my first diploma. As a woman you will never quite measure up in football skills" (Knoppers & Elling, 1999, p. 22). Although such standards also exclude some men from certification courses, there are relatively more men than women who are admitted and who receive their diplomas (Timmer, 1995). Admittance to the course that prepares coaches to coach professional football, for example, is limited to those who have played it at that level. This limitation excludes all women. A woman coach explains: "As a woman you are not allowed to take the course that qualifies you for coaching professional football because you have never played [men's] professional football" (Knoppers & Bouman 1996, p. 40). Obviously then, certification courses create levels of differentiation that are often congruent with gender.

SKEWNESS AS A NONISSUE

The neutral meanings assigned to performance means that these coaches tend to see the skewed gender ratio in coaching as a nonissue. Most of the coaches say that anyone who wishes to become a coach can do so; they agree that a policy of meritocracy prevails in the naming of coaches for the higher-level women's and men's teams. A male coach says: "I do not know if it is desirable or necessary to have more women coaches. We currently have a male coach [for our women's team] and a female chaperone. That works well" (Knoppers & Bouman, 1996, p. 90). Another coach argues that "the lack of women coaches is not really a problem because no one suffers if they are coached by a man" (Knoppers & Bouman, 1998, p. 100). Both men and women hold this view. In general, women coaches who participated in these studies perceive no obstacles that prevent them from achieving their goals. A woman coach explains the skewed gender ratio in the following way: "Nothing has stood in my way . . . I think it is the fault of women themselves" (Knoppers & Bouman, 1996; p. 87). Another woman coach says: "I think it is women who discriminate and not men; it does not matter to men if you are a woman or a man [as coach]" (Knoppers & Bouman, 1996, p. 87).

The only coaches who see gender as an issue are women in higher (paid) coaching positions.[3] They are the ones who describe negative experiences and attribute them to gender. A woman who coaches top-level korfball recounts: "I hear them say things about me. They say 'what a guy! ' Or, 'that bitch has a big mouth'. You learn to ignore them but it is not pleasant. I do not like to be seen in such a negative manner" (Knoppers & Bouman, 1996, p. 98). Two-thirds of these elite women coaches think they have to be better than men to obtain a higher (paid) coaching position. One of them explains: "As a woman you have to be able to eat iron if you want to be known as a good coach" (Knoppers & Elling, 1999, p. 27). Another says: "Women don't get to coach at the top because men do not want them there and have difficulty accepting them" (Knoppers & Bouman, 1996, p. 77). A woman coach of an elite team says: "I get tired of having to prove myself every time. In that respect I wish I were a man. They have it much easier in this football world" (Knoppers & Bouman, 1996; p. 98). Male coaches confirm this. A man explains why a male coach will always be chosen for the first men's team of his football club. "There is always a possibility that it does not click between a woman coach and the team and we cannot risk that" (Knoppers & Bouman, 1996, p. 77).

DOMESTIC DIFFERENTIATION

Although coaches frequently say that meritocratic practices ensure that gender is not an issue in coaching, their explanations of the skewed gender ratio tend to equate gender with women and to attribute part of the skewness to women's domestic responsibilities. In this respect, they openly engage in differentiation. A male coach explains that "Dutch women are responsible for child rearing; raising children and conducting swimming practices do not go together" (Knoppers & Bouman, 1998, p. 108). Another man explains how decisions are often made: "Women usually choose for the children because men earn more than women. My work does not allow me to work less than full-time. So my partner stopped with her [paid] work and sport involvement and chose for the children" (Knoppers & Bouman, 1996, p. 29). Similarly a man explains: "We agreed that one of us would stay home with the children; it didn't matter who it was, her or me. We agreed that she should stay home because she earned a third of what I earned. These are very simple choices!" (Knoppers & Bouman, 1998, p. 94).

Relatively speaking, men showed little understanding that much of their sport labor is made possible only by the work of their women partners. Many male coaches expect female colleagues to invest as much time as they themselves are able to do. They tend to see their women colleagues as falling short in their devotion to coaching yet fail to see that they compare women coaches to themselves and their domestic arrangements. They attribute their personal household arrangement to free choice and economic forces. They see these arrangements as self-evident and gender neutral. Interestingly, women who work in small part-time jobs mention time constraints more often than women who work full-time. The part time workers talk about having to stop doing volunteer work in sport because they are too busy running the household. In contrast, a male coach recounts how he is looking forward to becoming a *house man* (a stay at home Dad) next year because then he will have time to coach! Obviously men and women give different meanings to the concept of household responsibility.

Of course there are male coaches who do recognize their own responsibilities and privileges. These tend to be men, often very active in sport, who are married to women who have a long history of being involved in sport. Women coaches describe how that works. "The whole weekend we are on the [football] field. My son and boyfriend also play . . .My whole family participates in sport" (Knoppers & Bouman, 1996, p. 58). Another woman explains how she and her husband cope: "My husband likes to ride his motorcycle and I enjoy coaching a korfball team, so we both have something we like to do. We decided that our two children may not suffer from our activities so we take turns to ensure that one of us is always at home" (Knoppers & Bouman, 1998, p. 30). A woman coach points out that the spouses of male coaches tend to stay home and stop their sport involvement because those who are involved in sport are often more conservative than the rest of society. "The women in our club are not liberated. The club membership does not reflect society" (Knoppers & Bouman, 1998, p. 108).

PERFORMANCE AND MALE NORMATIVITY

Making sense of meritocracy dominates these interviews with Dutch coaches in ten different sports as they try to explain the skewed gender ratio in coaching. Most of the interviewed coaches argue that gender plays no role in the selection, experiences and evaluation of coaches nor in the creation of club culture. In other words, they frame meanings given to performance in a gender neutral way. Consequently, they see their sport club, organization, or association as places that are accessible and that offer equal opportunities to all who wish to coach. They contend that the best person is usually selected for a (top) coaching position and that gender rarely plays a role in this selection. The justification of inequity by using meanings given to performance is not unique to Dutch coaches, however. This viewpoint receives much support. Dutch sport journalists use the same argument to defend the scarcity of coverage given to women's sport (Knoppers & Elling, 2004). Dutch sport administrators and officials also use similar arguments to defend the lack of ethnic minorities in their clubs and the limiting of resources for girls and women (Knoppers & Anthonissen, 2001). Similar findings have been documented in Canadian, Australian, American, Finnish, and English sport (Hall, Cullen & Slack, 1990; McKay, 1997; 1999; Knoppers, 1992; Raivo, 1986; White & Brackenridge, 1985). These researchers conclude that a main barrier to bringing about change in the ratio of men to women and in the hegemonic male culture in sport is the failure of those in positions of leadership in organizations to see inequality as an issue. These leaders tend to see sport organizations as places of equal opportunity where performance erases skin color and gender and is objectively measured by outcome. In other words, sport is assumed to erase societal differences. In this sense, the findings mirror a global discourse about gender and sport. Yet the power of these meanings to shape gender in Dutch sport may be partially contextual as well.

The shape and power of the perception that sport is a place of equal opportunity may be unique to Dutch sport in several ways. First, Dutch sport clubs are voluntary organizations. The accessibility and opportunities for women and girls at such clubs is not explicitly addressed in any laws forbidding discrimination. The campaigns and programs that have been used by government agencies and several sport organizations to improve female involvement in sport primarily use persuasion. Compliance is voluntary. In addition, the voluntary nature of the club system means that individuals seemingly have a free choice whether or not to join a specific club. This perception of free choice may reinforce associations between sport and meritocracy in the Netherlands and in any country where sport is organized in a voluntary club system. This perception may mitigate change since individuals tend not to join clubs where they feel unwelcome (Elling, de Knop & Knoppers, 2003). Second, since on the average the coaches in the current study are experienced and certified, they have invested considerable time and effort in the current system. Some even coach in the sport club where they were involved as a young athlete. The visibility of women athletes and a few women coaches in every sport, especially at the youth sport level, may be construed as evidence that women have equal opportunities in sport if they want them. Consequently these Dutch coaches may have internalized the meritocracy discourse about sport, gender and equal opportunity and see their ideas as common sense. In addition, those who do not see Dutch sport as a gender neutral site for meritocracy may have dropped out of coaching and/or not wish to spend time, energy and money to become certified.

As the current data indicate, a perception of gender-neutrality favors men and uses them as norm. The finding that women coaches are seen in a positive light when they adhere to the standard of the ideal male is not just limited to Dutch sport. Hargreaves (1994, p. 203) argues in her description of gender and English sport that "when women are appointed to leadership positions [in sport], it is usually because they have demonstrated those values and ways of behaving that are essentially masculinist and confrontational" (p. 203). Similarly Coakley (1998), in a critical analysis of gender and American sport, asserts that "women get jobs only when they present compelling objective evidence of their qualifications, combined with other evidence that they can do things the way successful men have done them in the past" (p. 228). This norm is linked to meanings given to sport performance. It reflects Lorber's (1993) argument that when sport is defined primarily in terms of quantified best performance and that when what counts as sport is primarily limited to those activities where men excel, the performances and behaviors of elite male athletes become the abstract standard. Women's bodies are then given meanings that make them inferior to men's bodies which makes inequity in terms of programs and resources seem justified.

IGNORANCE OF DOMESTIC SUPPORT

The use of male as norm extends to domestic support for sport involvement. These coaches seem to take the amount of time many men have available to be active in sport organizations as the norm so that coaching responsibilities are defined accordingly. They attribute the under-representation of women coaches in part to their domestic responsibilities. There is little or no recognition that most men are able to be active in sport organizations only because they have a supportive (usually female) partner who takes on the bulk of *their* domestic work. This finding is not unique to Dutch sport, however, but is generally part of the structure of both paid and voluntary organizational work in the Western world. Organizations tend to have a gendered structure that assumes that both work and leisure are separate from domestic life and that ignores the interdependence between paid/volunteer work, leisure and domestic work (Boyle & McKay, 1995; Deem, 1986; Connell, 1987). The invisibility of the domestic support most men receive impacts the occupational structure of coaching in another way as well. Men, who enjoy such domestic support but do not see it as such, also often occupy positions of leadership in sport organizations where they are involved in making decisions about child care, about the extent of a coach's responsibilities, about required time involvement, etc. As Reskin (1988) argues "the dominant groups remain privileged because they write the rules and the rules they write, enable them to continue to write the rules" (p. 60).

The emphasis on and belief in meritocracy and gender-neutrality despite the use of the experiences, behaviors and life situation of a specific group of males as norm, is an example of fragmentation. Yet it is not recognized as such since the emphasis is on consensus. Meritocracy is assumed to prevail and perceived to be gender blind. The under-representation of women in high positions was primarily attributed to reasons located in women themselves such as lack of motivation or ability and having responsibilities for child rearing and household.

Benschop (1996), who found similar results in a study of gender in occupations in the Dutch banking world, explains this belief in gender blindness and gender neutrality by arguing that social desirability and social practice are often assumed to be the same. She contends that "values and norms about equality are presented as practices of equality, which means that the ways in which meanings given to gender differences in organizations are hidden" (p. 272). Thus the implicit use of ideal males as norm becomes invisible in the sport setting. The coaches involved in these studies tend to see both themselves and sport as neutral and objective and thus they may have equated this desirability with social reality. Their discourse of gender neutrality and meritocracy stands in sharp contrast to their frequent use of a misogynist discourse however.

MEANINGS OF MALE DOMINANCE
AND FEMALE DEVALUATION

VALUING THE PERFORMANCE OF MEN

Generally, women must be outstanding to succeed in obtaining their coaching diplomas. There is little room for mediocre women as there may be for mediocre men. Women coaches and officials "constantly have to prove themselves" (Knoppers & Bouman, 1996, p. 75). An instructor of a certification course recounts:

> I teach a certification course for coaches. Men and women take the same course and are evaluated the same way. The women are in the minority . . .While the skill levels of the men are quite diverse, all the women are usually very good (Knoppers & Bouman 1996, p. 75).

At the same time, complex situations can evolve when the required high skill level of women coaches challenges the prevailing gender logic and creates ambiguity. A football coach recounts how she fared during a course that prepares coaches to coach elite teams.

> There were 20 men and one woman involved in the course. I was better than most of the other students which led to irritation. My marks were kept low. This was also obvious at the last oral exam. I knew more about the topic than the instructor. I passed but they did not dare to give me a higher grade than most of the men (Knoppers & Bouman, 1996, p. 18).

Another woman who completed a high level coaching certification course in athletics recounts that "you could see that the men tried to go faster because they could not stand it that a female beat them. They did not say anything but you could see it happening" (Knoppers & Bouman, 1998, p. 128).

Coaches who participated in these studies link men with best performance to imply that women athletes and coaches are inferior/subordinate because they will never be able to perform like men. A woman coach describes how this inference impacts her work: "The sport administrators and the team supporters are much more critical of a woman than they are of a man coach. Because I have to prove myself much more than a man has to, I have to put much energy into that" (Knoppers & Bouman 1998, p. 98). A woman coach recounts how she was not considered for a coaching position although she had earned the requisite coaching certificate: "A sport administrator of Club X let the top men's team go without a coach for half a year while I was available and had the necessary qualifications. He was looking for a male coach" (Knoppers & Bouman 1998, p. 36).

VALUING THE BEHAVIOR OF MEN

Not only has the physicality/performance of skilled male athletes become the norm but other aspects associated with athletic masculinities also have become the standard by which everyone is evaluated. A coach describes how this standard can translate into ambiguous practices: "A woman took the certification course. She did very well. We treated her as if she were a man" (Knoppers & Elling, 1999, p. 32). Similarly, women who show qualities associated with the preferred masculinity, are complimented: "Those women hockey coaches have obviously competed at the top level . . .they always want to win; it is really the mentality of men and I like that" (Knoppers & Bouman, 1996, p. 94). Some coaches say that they like working with lesbian athletes because of their high levels of performance and their "male mentality" (p. 94). They are defined as being like men and are assumed to be physically stronger and mentally tougher than straight women. A male football coach explains: "If you have a lesbian and a 'normal' girl, then the lesbian will be a better football player, she will have better skills. Lesbians are like males" (Knoppers & Bouman, 1996, p. 94).

Obviously, these coaches tend to compare women coaches to the idealized image of certain types of athletic males. Occasionally a minority alternate discourse is used that does not have a male as implicit starting point. For example, a few women coaches have developed successful self-presentation strategies that differ from the male-identified norm. A woman coach uses whispering as one of her ways of communicating with players in contrast to the yelling and screaming she sees other [male] coaches use. She says that when she whispers, the members of her men's team really have to listen to her (Knoppers & Bouman, 1996, p. 43). Another describes how she handles sexist remarks: "I pretend I do not understand what they are saying. It is like teaching children. When they do not display the desired behavior then you act as if you do not understand them. You ignore it and reward good behavior and that usually works" (Knoppers & Bouman, 1996, p. 88). The use of such techniques seems to be rare however. Most male and female coaches try to show desired masculine behavior but label it as neutral. This use of male as norm impacts how women, and behavior associated with women, are seen.

DEVALUATION OF 'WOMANLY'

Regardless of type of sport, women are most likely to coach youth, women and lower skilled teams (Knoppers & Bouman, 1996; 1998; Knoppers & Elling, 2001). A highly qualified woman coach describes her experiences: "The top [male] athletes of the club do not accept you because you are a woman . . . Now I work with the highly skilled youth" (Knoppers & Bouman, 1998, p. 82). The devaluation of women and of behaviors associated with what they see as 'womanly' is an often mentioned topic when these coaches discuss gender and sport. They frequently distance and differentiate themselves from what they see as 'womanly' such as the showing of certain emotions and behaviors that are assumed to interfere with elite performance. "They [women] cry at the most unexpected moments. It is always yakkety yak . . . you have to watch what you say to them" (Knoppers & Bouman, 1996, p. 93). A male coach describes the members of his athletic team: "They [girls] have all sorts of things wrong with them but I just ignore that. They are like adolescents; the boys are not so bad. The girls are quite bitchy" (Knoppers & Bouman, 1996, p. 93). Another man thinks women are difficult to coach because "if you have to coach eight to ten women someone's hormone cycle will always interfere . . . pffff" (Knoppers & Bouman, 1998, p. 133).

Women athletes are described by women and men coaches as weaker/ less skilled than men, as whiners with little mental toughness, as fighting like cats, as holding grudges for a long time, and, as being jealous of each other. A male coach concludes: "There is nothing worse than a team of women. Yes, they do nothing but provoke and nag each other" (Knoppers & Bouman, 1998, 135). Men are described as being competitive with each other which is assumed to make them better athletes, as working out disagreements in a physical or verbal manner that immediately clears the air, and, as doing assigned tasks without 'whining'. A male coach explains that

> men are direct, straightforward, and quick to laugh; their fights with each other occur at the surface and are rapidly solved; the disagreements among women occur at a deeper level so you do not know what is going on. You have to prod and keep asking which is very tiring. They can become quite mean (Knoppers & Bouman, 1996; p. 93).

When men are perceived to act like women, their actions are interpreted in a negative way as well. A male coach of a senior men's team says: "I now have some 'old wives' on my team . . . to put it bluntly . . . all they do is gab . . . that is what usually happens on a girls' team" (Knoppers & Bouman, 1996, p. 93). Women coaches engage in this devaluation as if they themselves are not women. They talk about women as 'they' and like it when they themselves are seen as 'one of the men.' A woman coach who performs gender successfully by such standards, proudly recounts how she was a "man among men" when she coached a senior male team. "They told such awful jokes that they never would have told if there had been women present " (Knoppers & Bouman, 1996, p. 94).

A few men and women do not see women as subordinate but argue that women athletes are more motivated and more eager to learn than men athletes are. A woman coach recounts for example, how male athletes prefer to be coached by her instead of her male colleagues because her training sessions are more enjoyable and because she pays more attention to them as individuals (Knoppers & Bouman, 1998; p. 135). Another argues that girls are more eager to learn than boys who think they know it all (Knoppers & Bouman, 1998, pp. 137-138). These coaches are the exception however. In general, coaches are negative about women coaches and athletes and the behaviors they associate with them.

The giving of meanings is never a straightforward and linear process however, but often contains contradictory and ambiguous elements. These coaches sometimes contradict themselves within the same interviews. For example, a woman coach says "I am against stereotypes." Later she says that "perseverance is a male quality, going on until you drop. Women do not do that at all. Being sly and bitchy are female qualities" (Knoppers & Bouman, 1996, p. 95). Regardless of contradictions and alternate discourses that are part of the interview data, the themes of neutrality and male normativity are a constant and dominant factor that frames the discourse these coaches employ to explain the skewed gender ratio in coaching.

PREFERRED FORMS OF MASCULINITY

The overall view these coaches seem to have about women is that many women have little to contribute to the sport world because they rarely measure up to that that is associated with desirable masculinities. These coaches tend to value women primarily when they behave in accordance with images of skilled men.

The dominant negative image and devaluation of women that emerges from these interviews reflects Meyerson & Kolb's (2000) conclusion that managerial masculinities continue to be socially constructed as "the ostensibly neutral standard against which femininity is constructed as 'other'" (p. 562). The practice of managerial work also differentiates among social groups by subordinating what is associated with women, marginalizing gay men and bestowing a patriarchal dividend on certain groups of men (Connell, 1987; 1995).

The degree of devaluation of what is associated with 'womanly' may differ across societal area. Although women may be subordinated in many areas of society, their devaluation may possibly be stronger in sport, especially in sports that are associated with men and with which men and boys identify in order to create a desirable masculine identity for themselves (see for example Connell, 1995; Messner, 1992; Pascoe, 2003). Frequently, an identification with this desirable masculinity means differentiation from what one associates with womanly (Whitehead, 2002).

Sport can connect men and boys to definitions of masculinity in which a major rule is a repudiation of all that is associated with females (Kimmel, 1999). This is reinforced through admonitions that "you are playing like a bunch of girls" or that "you throw like a girl" and exhortations to "take it like a man", to be tough, etc.

Messner (1988) has argued that although the resistance to female athletes may be decreasing, the effort to keep sport associated with a certain type of masculinity and not with what is currently defined as 'feminine', influences meanings given to positions of leadership so that males are seen as the most logical candidates for such positions. Hovden (2000), in a study of gendering processes in the selection of leaders in Norwegian sport organizations, for example, found that selection discourses are congruent with images of heroic corporate leadership skills.

Images about coaching and other forms of leadership in sports tend to be seen "in terms that are consistent with traditional ideas about masculinity: if you 'coach like a girl' you are doing it wrong; if you 'coach like a man, ' you are doing it right" (Coakley, 2004, p. 256). Moodley (1999), in a summary of the literature about masculinity, contends that the devaluation of that what is associated with females is common to many definitions of masculinity. Whitehead and Barrett (2001) agree and describe masculinities as "those behaviors, languages and practices, existing in specific cultural and organizational locations, which are commonly associated with males and thus culturally defined as not feminine" (pp. 15 -16). Dutch sport therefore is a site where this differentiation is reinforced by gendered meanings given to positions of leadership.

UNDERSTANDING THE CONTEXT SPECIFICITY OF GENDER AND COACHING

Interestingly with few exceptions, both men and women coaches involved in these studies are complicit in this devaluation of women. This finding differs somewhat from similar studies on gender and sport leadership in other countries (see for example, Hall, Cullen & Slack, 1990; Knoppers, 1992; Moore, Parkhouse & Konrad, 2001; White & Brackenridge, 1985; Macintosh & Whitson, 1989). In such studies women were more likely than men to name inequities and to argue for change. In the current Dutch studies this pattern occurs only among coaches of elite teams. The complicity of the majority of the women coaches with the devaluation of women seems to be unique to the Dutch situation and may in part reflect the strength and power of the intersections of meritocratic discursive practices, the voluntary structure of Dutch sport, and, degree of societal misogyny.

In countries like the USA where sport is part of educational institutions, laws like Title IX require gender equity in sport. Schools must provide similar sport opportunities and resources for women and men. Title IX has been instrumental in motivating schools to provide males and females with equal opportunities and resources to compete in sport. Since the educational values of sport participation play a role in justifying sport programs in a school curriculum, it is difficult to justify excluding half the population from opportunities to learn those values. In contrast, the basis of Dutch sport, like that in many European countries, is the local club. Since clubs are private entities and memberships are voluntary, clubs are not legally required to provide opportunities for girls and women. It is possible then, that the meanings given to gender and coaching are specific to a societal setting such as the Netherlands and in the USA. Women's successful participation as leaders in the current Dutch sport seems to require complicity with certain masculinities that require differentiation from what is associated with 'womanly', although there is evidence of limited individual resistance. Relatively little research has been conducted on the intersection of this dynamic with the degree to which that that is associated with women is devaluated in Dutch society as a whole.

DISCUSSION AND CONCLUSION

An assumption underlying feminist analyses of organizational discursive practices is that meanings that are presented as neutral in dominant discourses often contain a gender logic that implicitly and explicitly produces and reproduces social group differentiation (see for example, Acker, 1990; 1992; 2000; Benschop, 1996).

On the surface, such discursive practices may seem to be gender-free and yet they have a gendered impact. Acker (1992) says: "What is problematic is the discontinuity, even contradiction, between organizational realities obviously structured around gender and ways of thinking and talking about these same realities as though they were gender neutral" (p. 255). Although the ways in which this discontinuity is expressed in the current data may be unique to the Dutch sport situation, the construction of the association between gender and so-called objective measures is not unique to sport nor the Dutch situation.

Kerfoot & Knights (1998) argue that the construction of excellence in performance as an objective and therefore rational norm, results in defining behavior associated with women as weak, emotional and irrational. In other words, an emphasis on what are assumed to be objective measures may be a discursive practice associated with certain masculinities. Van Zoonen (1989) makes the same argument in discussing objectivity and journalism. She points out that a masculinity that is characterized by detachment and rationality is a hidden and often denied component of an emphasis on objectivity. By using what they call objective criteria in their processes of sense making about gender, coaches can view themselves as detached outsiders, may subordinate that what they associate with 'womanly' and, have no responsibility for gender inequities because they do not perceive them as such. Thus, in this implicit way, differentiation and integration occur simultaneously in sense making of the skewed gender ratio in coaching.

As I pointed out at the beginning of this chapter, coaches have a direct working relationship with athletes and have a visible position of leadership. Their discursive practices impact athletes directly. Since almost all coaches are former athletes, coaches play a crucial role in perpetuating and challenging dominant discourses in sport. The strength of these discourses suggests that changing them may be a difficult task.

Notes

[1] In the Netherlands, men occupy more positions of leadership in sport organizations (89.7 %) than in other volunteer organizations (79.6 %) (Emancipatieraad, 1997). About 80% of the coaches and 91% of Dutch sport administrators and officials are men (Emancipatieraad, 1997; Stol, 1995). Although football is the fastest growing sport for girls, 99 % of the 10,000 certified football coaches are men (Pauw, 2000; Stol, 1995).

[2] With few exceptions, men and women present and use the same themes in similar ways. Consequently, I categorize the data by gender or sport only where differences occur. I use quotes that best illustrate a certain viewpoint and present contradictions wherever they exist.

[3] Elite coaches comprised five percent of all women participating in these studies.

CHAPTER 6
"I'M BEYOND THE DISCRIMINATION PHASE":
CONSTRUCTING ETHNIC IDENTITY IN FOOTBALL

Paul Verweel and Anton Anthonissen

"A look, a tone, a movement of the body can be hurtful." (Astrid Roemer cited in Van Hoek & Van Veen, 1997, p. 9)

OVERVIEW

The following article appeared in a city newspaper[1]:

Kamalo Balo fails to finish a match

> The game White Orange – Kamalo Balo in the second division of the region Utrecht got out of hand yesterday. The referee Diks ended the match nine minutes before the end with the score 2-1, after a huge fight broke out among the Surinam players of Kamalo Balo and the Dutch home team. Adri van Dalem of White Orange is crystal clear about who caused the violence: Kamalo Balo. Errol Groeneveld, coach of the Kamalo Balo team, places the blame for the violence on the referee Diks and Arne Peypers, the goalie for White Orange. Van Dalem: "Our goalie made a brilliant save in the cross after which he was roughed up. Those crooks are quick to use their fists. A Kamalo Balo fan chased one of our players with a knife that was 30 cm. long. Luckily the chair of our club was able to prevent escalation of the incident." Van Dalem added that he would send an angry letter to the KNVB [Royal Dutch Football Association].
> Groeneveld, the coach of Kamalo Balo, felt that the referee had failed to do his job. "I think the referee left home with the idea of making it difficult for Kamalo Balo. I continually told the boys to calm down which worked until number 4 of White Orange pushed Geronimo Edwards. The goalie left the goal to come to his brother's defense. He began to hit and kick my player." Groeneveld did not consider it a rough contest. "Football is our sport. We will probably get the blame. No, I am far beyond the discrimination phase. Every week we compete against 13 people. If it continues like this, we should consider withdrawing from the competition." According to Klarenbeek, chair of the referees' committee, neither the referee nor his supervisor saw anything. "No, we are not so happy with that. The referee felt threatened and recommended that the police be called. This will be a difficult case for the Discipline Committee. I do not see Kamalo Balo as a club of trouble makers." (*Utrecht Nieuwsblad*, 27 November 1995).

Kamalo Balo was founded in 1961 as a football club by a group of Surinam-Dutch athletes in a suburb of Utrecht. By 1995 it had a total of six boys'/men's football teams and had become a multicultural club with members who have roots in Surinam, Morocco, Poland and Spain and a few in the Netherlands. Outsiders still see it as a Surinam- Dutch club, however. We are familiar with the background of Kamalo Balo and reflected on the content of the article in the newspaper since it is an account of a fight. As scholars and as athletes, we have seen and heard this before. We assume that the quotes in the article accurately reflect what was said. Something was probably said during the match; someone was kicked or punched and beaten without the referee seeing it and it gets out of hand. Kamalo Balo talks about mitigating circumstances. We recognize the denial of the seriousness of the situation and the shifting of blame to the victims or the referee. Board members of sport clubs will never admit that their team or club misbehaved or violated the rules. We have experienced the same thing ourselves. But then we see the name of Errol Groeneveld. We know him and know that he is an honest person. If he says that the official was at fault then we cannot blame Kamalo Balo. Suddenly various meanings based on different frames such as our own sport experiences, our disbelief in the denials made by the fighters from Kamalo Balo, and, our knowledge of Errol, collide. We now doubt the connection we made between the incident and the first frame we used to interpret it.

RESEARCH QUESTION AND METHODOLOGY

The newspaper article describes an incident between an immigrant and nonimmigrant club but we know little of the extent to which ethnicity is assigned a role in the account.[2] Did the witnesses see a knife because they expected one when they saw athletes whom they label as immigrants? Possibly the referee was wrong or perhaps this was an incident of discrimination. The discrepancy in assignment of meanings to the incident motivated us to explore the incident using the following research question:

How does the use of various frames of meanings color the ways in which ethnicity is constructed in the Kamalo Balo incident?

We received permission from Kamalo Balo to explore the extent to which the created image of a highly volatile club whose fans carry knives is congruent with the culture of Kamalo Balo. After receiving approval from the club's board, we conducted 35 interviews with male board members, coaches, members of the first team and other members, observed the club in action, and, followed twenty matches of the top men's team for a year.[3]

FRAMES FOR SENSE MAKING

THE IMMIGRANT CLUB AS FRAME

The framing of the incident involves the sport, political and societal meanings at the individual, structural and social levels. Kamalo Balo is a Surinam - Dutch club and tends to be labeled as an immigrant club. Both the labels of immigrant and nonimmigrant are fuzzy concepts that function as abstract frames that create a place for the actual clubs themselves (Weick, 1995). These fuzzy concepts mask a diversity of national and ethnic differences among the athletes. Members of an immigrant club consisting primarily of people from Surinam have as little in common with each other as do members of a nonimmigrant factory club, a Christian club or a white Dutch rural club.

Currently 10 percent of the Dutch population is described as immigrant (Breedveld, 2003). Most (93%) of the immigrant athletes are either members of a nonimmigrant club or train or play without being part of a club. Only 7% are members of an immigrant sport club.[4] A majority (90%) of the respondents of a survey conducted in Rotterdam are negative about the existence of immigrant sport clubs (Duyvendak, 1998).

They favor only temporary immigrant clubs. The responses of the immigrants who participated in this study show that 17% of them prefer to be members of an immigrant club while 30% prefer a mixed ethnic club. The remainder did not indicate a preference. Obviously most of the nonimmigrant and immigrant population prefer sport clubs to be 'integrated.'

Why then do Kamalo Balo members want their own club? A player explains:

> In the Netherlands, you are seen as someone from Surinam, not as Dutch. And then it is very frustrating to describe yourself as Dutch. Often you are forced to face these facts, which is difficult. I am ambivalent about this. I feel more Surinam than Dutch (Swank 1996, p. 10).

A board member says: "You begin to talk about 'us' and 'they' and to behave accordingly. The danger in stuff like this is that you begin to believe things that really do not exist" (Swank 1996, p. 10). Another member explains that

> the negative treatment of black players by the spectators has been going on for a long time. Clubs haven't done anything about this for years so they shouldn't be so hypocritical. For years they have created and allowed this [anti-black] culture to develop" (Swank 1996, p. 11).

Swank (1996) concludes that discrimination within and outside sport creates feelings and emotions that are reason enough for immigrant athletes to set up their own clubs so that they can participate in sport in their own circle.[5]

In other words, when Dutch athletes with a Turkish, Moroccan, Surinam or Antillean background start their own club they do so because of because of their negative experiences elsewhere. This motivation is often judged negatively by nonimmigrants who feel that separate clubs are undesirable (Anthonissen 2000; Janssens, 1998; Elling & de Knop, 1999).

Experiences (cues) clash in the sense making in which they frame sport. Meanings that evolve out of sense making of sporting practices in which skin color and ethnicity lead to categorization clash with the dominant sport discourse that in sport only performance matters (Knoppers & Anthonissen 2001). In other words, the construction of meanings at the personal level clash with ideas about how sport should be structured.

THE POLITICAL FRAME

Politicians and social scientists have described Dutch society as segmented (see for example, Siebers, Verweel & De Ruijter 2002). As Verweel and Knoppers have described in Chapter 1, various societal groups used to organize themselves in separate societies or *pillars* (such as Roman Catholic, Protestant and secular; working class and upper class). Each pillar had its own system of education, sport clubs, churches, and ideology and was represented in parliament and in national sport organizations. In other words, the organization of Dutch society and the categorization of its people were based on religious and societal ideologies. Gradually these pillars have shrunk although they have not yet lost their influence (Entzinger, 2004). The negative attitudes that nonimmigrants have toward the establishment of separate sport clubs tend to ignore this history. In addition, the Dutch constitution gives everyone the right to freely organize; in other words it allows voluntary organizations based on difference. Setting up a separate sport club based on an ethnic category is therefore a right and a historically common social practice.

Large groups of colonial immigrants with roots in Surinam, the Dutch Antilles or Indonesia began to come to the Netherlands in the 1950s; other immigrants were recruited for menial labor from Morocco, Turkey and China in the 1960s and 1970s. These immigrants and others who came to the Netherlands before the 1980s encountered this pillarization and were also categorized into groups based on their country of origin.

Each group was treated differently in the areas of welfare, education and sport on the assumption that their countries of origin differed as well. Little attention was paid to heterogeneity within such ethnic groups. Twenty-five years later those policies have changed. The focus on differences has been replaced with an emphasis on ethnic integration (Rapport integratiebeleid minderheden, 2003). This means that although immigrant clubs are legal, they now tend to be seen as undesirable. Nonimmigrant people have concluded that separate clubs do not enhance ethnic integration.

References to ethnic integration in sport policies usually imply that immigrants should participate in nonimmigrant clubs so that they have the opportunity to interact and mix with nonimmigrants (Burgers, et al., 1998). The degree of integration is subsequently measured by the degree to which immigrants assimilate the Dutch way of practicing, competing and organizing sport in general, and, the club in particular (Duyvendak, 1999). An assimilated male or female immigrant competing for a nonimmigrant club is someone who contributes to the level of performance of the club, who plays the sport the way the Dutch do, who does volunteer work for the club and who speaks Dutch well.

In other words, an assimilated immigrant is one who resembles nonimmigrants. Assimilation has become the goal of national policies that focus on ethnic integration. Government officials and sport leaders assume that ethnic integration in sport also enhances or facilitates the ethnic integration of immigrants in other segments of society (Elling, De Knop & Knoppers, 2001; Lagendijk & van der Gugten, 1996; Janssens, 1998). They often hope and assume that sport participation by immigrants reduces the crime rate and prevents them from becoming societal dropouts.

SOCIETAL FRAMES

The question about the definition of ethnic integration is not just confined to sport but is part of a larger question about societal participation of immigrants in all levels of Dutch society. The government contends that having a job is one of the most important societal markers of ethnic integration in the Netherlands (Vermeulen & Penninx, 2000). Entry into the labor market requires learning the language, acquiring common social interaction skills, adopting the dominant values and norms of nonimmigrants, and, possessing certain skills and experiences. Education and schooling are seen as prerequisites for obtaining and keeping a job. A current societal debate centers on the approach to cultural differences within immigrants groups and between immigrants and nonimmigrants. Should immigrants be required to assimilate as much as possible? Do they have the right to segregation that allows them to be different? Do they have a right to live in a multi-cultural society in which differences are accepted outside their own circles and are seen as adding value to society? While some scholars emphasize ethnic integration in the form of assimilation, other scholars point to the value of multiculturalism in which differences are coordinated (Anthonissen & van Eekeren, 2000; de Ruijter, 1995; Entzinger, 1998 Roosevelt, 1993; Verweel, 2001).

Three societal frames are commonly used to examine the participation of immigrants in the labor market: deficiency, cultural complexity and discrimination (Glastra, 1996, 2001).
   • The deficiency frame is most popular and assumes that immigrants are deficient in the Dutch language and in other skills needed to function well in the Dutch labor market. Consequently, they are taught these skills and the Dutch language so that they can be similar to the nonimmigrants. The deficiency frame is therefore explicit part of the integration perspective on organizing diversity such is used in the chapters of this book.
   • The cultural complexity[6] frame assumes that both nonimmigrants and immigrants have to learn to handle the meaning of cultural differences. The use of this frame generally requires that individuals be educated about collective cultural differences and viewpoints. "The way in which people think and act is primarily explained and understood in terms of their original ethnic and national culture" (Glastra, 2001, p. 702). Verweel (Chapter 2) describe this as differentiation. Sometimes the cultural complexity frame is also used when ambiguity and individual differences seem to dominate the situation. Then it becomes part of a fragmentation perspective on coping with diversity (see also Chapter 2).
   • The discrimination frame searches for visible and hidden mechanisms in interpersonal actions, structures, and, organizational culture that reproduce unequal social relations between different ethnic groups and individuals. The use of this frame requires these barriers to be identified and removed through social processes and changes in discourses, regulations, functional positions and relations. The objective of this frame is to increase social diversity in organizational processes.

Little of these debates resound in the Dutch sport world (Anthonissen 2001; Knoppers & Anthonissen, 2001; Elling, De Knop & Knoppers, 2001). The deficiency frame, which is popular in debates about work, is rarely used with respect to sport skills since there is little controversy about the quality of the athletic skills of black male immigrants .[7] In fact, often nonimmigrant clubs recruit black immigrant men to help the men's first team to play at a higher level. In contrast, nonimmigrant players may feel deficient and perceive immigrant players as a threat. The deficiency frame therefore works in a positive manner for black male immigrants.

The lack of use of the deficiency frame in describing the participation of male immigrants in sport applies only to the athletes themselves however. The deficiency frame is often used to point to the shortcomings of immigrants, especially those from Turkish and Moroccan descent, in leadership and organizational abilities in sport (Knoppers & Anthonissen 2001). Specifically, immigrants are seen as deficient in matters such as paying membership fees on time, mentoring of younger players by older members, and, in complying with all the regulations of organizational life. Ironically, many nonimmigrant sport clubs have these same problems but do not frame them as a function of their nonimmigrant status.

The cultural complexity frame that requires individuals to learn to accept and work with collective and individual differences, tends to be used in the sport world only with respect to performances of athletes. Differences in playing style, especially those used by players with roots in the Dutch Antilles, Surinam and Indonesia, are not only accepted but as we indicated above, used to stereotype these players as very skilled. Black male immigrants, especially those from Surinam, are assumed to be highly skilled in football. Players with a Moroccan or Turkish background are stereotypically described as being quick and having a great sense of pride.

This stereotyping of the sporting abilities of male black-immigrants not only pertains to top football stars in the Netherlands such as Kluivert or Davids, but also for the elite players of Kamalo Balo who are playing at the seventh amateur level. This stereotyping of groups and individuals does not differ much from the ethnic/racial stereotyping that occurs in North American and British sport (see for example, McCarthy & Jones, 1997). Off the field however, differences between immigrants and nonimmigrants are expected to be negligible which means that all immigrants must assimilate in club life (Elling & de Knop, 1999; Elling, De Knop, & Knoppers (2001). In this way, the differentiation and deficiency perspectives overlap off the playing field.

The discrimination frame is used frequently in the sport world. Immigrant athletes feel that they are discriminated by nonimmigrants club members, referees and opponents; consequently they may be more focused on the reproduction of unequal social relations in sport. For example, the data concerning Kamalo Balo suggest that its members encounter referees who have a difficult time accepting the immigrant nature of the club. There are referees who do not want to hear any Surinam spoken on the field, who threaten the team at the beginning of the match with stopping it if there are problems, who give advantages to the other team, etc. We discovered in the first half-year of our research that individual experiences and incidents influenced the perspectives of the first men's team at Kamalo Balo even when they had excellent referees. Such experiences are based on personal histories and on seemingly insignificant behaviors as the quotation at the beginning of this chapter suggests. Incidents also occur within immigrant clubs that do not involve nonimmigrants. A member of Kamalo Balo says: "Some incidents have nothing to do with discrimination but more with temperament of the individuals involved" (Swank, 1996, p. 28). This last quotation illustrates the role a frame plays in the sense making of an incident.

Since sport is a half-open system, it is not surprising that immigrant athletes often place their experiences in sport in the context of their experiences of discrimination in the labor market and other organizations, in the media, in racist humor and in ethnocentric films such as Tarzan. Parents of nonimmigrant white athletes tend to see immigrant clubs as consisting primarily of volatile athletes, drug users and criminals.

Such assumptions and experiences frame, in part, the nature of the interactions in football matches. Many members of Kamalo Balo therefore, interpret their personal experiences (cues) within a discrimination frame. Such experiences range from the seemingly insignificant to highly charged emotional experiences. A Kamalo Balo member describes walking into a nonimmigrant club: "When you come inside, everyone suddenly sits and there is no place left to sit. People go sit in an empty corner" (Swank 1996, p. 14).

Other members of the Kamalo Balo club describe an emotional match: "The referee of a youth match was very difficult. The coach of Kamalo Balo decided to pull his team off the field because he could not guarantee their safety any longer. A parent of the opposing team scolded the coach using the term 'cancerous blacks.' The coach sprayed them with water from the water bottle. Six men beat him up. It is not the club but those parents" (Swank, 1996, p. 18).

Obviously then, the discrimination and deficiency frames are used by immigrant and nonimmigrant athletes and sport administrators to make sense of situation involving a combination of immigrants and nonimmigrants as athletes and sport officials. They tend not to use a cultural complexity frame that emphasizes ambiguity and individual differences and defines ethnic social positions in a complex and fragmented way.

EXPLAINING MEANINGS GIVEN TO KAMALO BALO

The economic, political and general societal context definitely influences sport participation and club life but does so within a specific situation. This situation is dominated by relational dynamics and the dominant frames used in sport and in the club itself (Anthonissen & Boessenkool, 1998). We explored this sport specific context and these dynamics at Kamalo Balo, a club described as an immigrant club.

We have argued earlier that THE Dutch immigrant club does not actually exist. This fuzzy category is too diverse in daily practice to yield meaningful descriptions. Sport clubs labeled as Surinam, Antillean, Moluccan, Turkish and/or Moroccan differ too much from each other. This analysis is therefore limited to the concrete situation in Kamalo Balo. We will look first at meanings given within the sport context, then at the social/organizational situation of the club, and, subsequently connect the two.

SPORT SPECIFIC MEANINGS

The referee whistles often, making many choices during a match. We notice that Kamalo Balo never reacts when the call goes against its team. In one match, for example, a totally wrong flag signal by the boundary official for Kamalo Balo is ignored. Neither team comments on this. There is no reaction when Kamalo Balo is not given two possible penalty situations. A player of Kamalo Balo is kicked hard by an opponent and lies hurt on the field. The opponents throw the ball back to Kamalo Balo because of the way the referee handles the injury and its cause. Kamalo Balo plays against an opponent with whom there had been problems previously. The opponents need to win this match if they wish to advance to a higher division. Before the match, an opponent hands a bouquet of flowers to the captain of Kamalo Balo to congratulate them on having advanced to the higher division already. The match could have been volatile but it develops in a peaceful manner although the boundary official of Kamalo Balo is ignored three times and a goal by Kamalo Balo is disallowed for unclear reasons (Verweel & David, 1995). These examples suggest that many situations occur during a game that require the use of frames to generate meanings about them. The insider frames tend to be narrowly focused whereas relatively detached outsiders like us may see other possible frames.

ORGANIZING THE CLUB

The Kamalo Balo club has a large social and sport function (Verweel & David, 1995). It is busy every day of the week, even when there are no sport events. The small restaurant/bar functions as a meeting place for various groups of men, women and youth, athletes and nonathletes alike. About 80 spectators attend home contests. The members of Kamalo Balo mirror the multi-ethnic nature of the Surinam population: Creoles, Hindus, Javanese, Indians and Chinese. Other members have their roots in the Dutch Antilles, Morocco, Spain and Poland. A few Dutch nonimmigrants are also members of the club. Members discovered the club through their networks. Many immigrant boys initially played for a nonimmigrant club and either did not make the first men's team or did not like it there. The few members who leave the club are the very talented boys who want to play at higher levels and repatriates who return to their country of origin.

The club has sufficient volunteers to fill all the technical, organizational and administrative positions. Board members regularly visit the bar, are spectators at the matches and/or coach a team. Board meetings are held once every four weeks and can be stormy. A board member says:
> Sometimes bad things happen in the council room . . . the things that are said!! But when we finish the meeting everything is OK again. We get along well with each other. You would never see two people in the bar with tension between them. We keep business and personal aspects separate" (Swank, 1997, p. 6).

Another member says that "we have a few hard working men in the council but sometimes they miscommunicate. This means that sometimes meetings are unnecessarily long" (Swank, 1996, p. 7). An agenda, to which points can be added, is used to conduct the meetings. Everyone's speaking time is limited. The club is in good shape financially although it took a while to achieve that status. The current board members have made agreements with those to whom they owe money and have agreed to abide by certain financial rules and regulations. The books are sound and healthy. This description of Kamalo Balo clearly shows that this is no problem club. In a certain sense, Kamalo Balo is like a typical nonimmigrant football club that highly values its social life. Kamalo Balo has a social value for those labeled as immigrant and is characterized by social ties that make it a hospitable club. The club is reasonably organized and plays good football. There are no indications of dangerous situations developing and potentially volatile situations are ignored.

CONNECTIONS

Our research debunks the image of Kamalo Balo as a dangerous club. How then can the uproar surrounding the incident described at the beginning of this chapter be explained? The answer can be found in what Weick (1995) says: "A cue in a frame is what makes sense, not a cue or a frame alone" (p. 111). As scholars, we use neither the deficiency nor the discrimination frame to study the club, but a more fragmented view. This means that we assign meanings to our observations that are different from those assigned by the participants in the incident. For example, the importance of cues and frames is illustrated in the incident with which we began this chapter. It is easy to dismiss this as just an incident. The members can only remember three such similar events in the last ten years. Yet everyone knows about this incident and that discrimination played a central role. The opponents (non immigrants) see the incident as confirming the image of Kamalo Balo members as fighters. Some will be certain that they saw a knife. They are using another frame to make sense of their experiences. This is quite different from the frames used by other immigrant clubs to talk about Kamalo Balo. Sometimes fights occur during those matches too, but they are not explained with the use of stereotypes. Any match can result in a fight but is always followed by a handshake; it has nothing to do with the club but only with fighters and football.

We see that it is the skin color of most of the Kamalo Balo members that frames the sense making or judgments made by nonimmigrant white Dutch athletes. The existence of immigrant sport clubs is judged negatively in and outside sport, which means that the focus is not on similarities but on collective differences between immigrant and nonimmigrant players. Skin color also enables Kamalo Balo members to make sense of such incidents by using primarily a discrimination frame. Positive experiences and incidents are quickly forgotten by the Kamalo Balo members so that a wrong look or remark can only be heard as an example of discrimination. Obviously, earlier feelings or experiences with discrimination in sport or outside sport, frame the sense making of these incidents by Kamalo Balo members. They are not the only ones to be selective in their use of frames however.

Politicians and government employees also tend use certain frames selectively. They find the old image of separate clubs each associated with a pillar undesirable because they argue that sport should not be categorized and organized on the basis of difference

(Anthonissen 2000; Janssens, 1998; Elling & de Knop, 1999; Elling, De Knop, & Knoppers (2001). They see sport as a place that should provide equal opportunity for everyone and assume that meanings given to performance in sport are objective and neutral (see Knoppers, Chapter 5). They tend to neglect the influence of societal tendencies towards ambiguity and individualization. Consequently, they rarely compare the multi-cultural character of Kamalo Balo with the heterogeneous and social membership profile of nonimmigrant clubs that are also organized along lines of social class, gender, sexual preference, age and ability (Anthonissen, 2001; Elling, 2002; Knoppers & Anthonissen, 2001). Policy makers and sport officials and administrators may find it difficult to recognize and accept this heterogeneity and resulting fragmentation because it complicates a functional way of organizing. Knoppers & Anthonissen address and expand on this topic in Chapter 8.

DISCUSSIONS AND CONCLUSION

Processes of differentiation and fragmentation obviously dominate sporting practices yet nonimmigrant athletes and immigrant and nonimmigrant policy makers continue to want and strive for ethnic integration defining it primarily in terms of assimilation (Rapport integratiebeleid minderheden, 2003). An alternate frame is needed to manage sense making of such situations: organizing diversity.

An organizing diversity frame starts with a desire for and possibility of a recognition and acceptance of differences between and within nonimmigrant and immigrant sport clubs. Differentiation between and within sport clubs, sports and individuals is seen as an expression of fragmentation. Individuals and sport organizations need this fragmentation to develop their own identity/meaning in relationship to the other, including their own ethnicity. In other words, individuals and organizations need the other to define themselves as persons, as athletes and as sport club. Social forces such as ethnicity /race, gender and class play a role in organizing and give meanings to personal identity and the identity of others (Knoppers & Anthonissen 2001; Anthonissen 2004). When these differences are coordinated instead of integrated they create a variety of frames for working with diversity. In the organizational literature the responsibility for this coordination is often assigned to management and therefore called diversity management (Kamp & Hagedoorn-Rasmussen, 2004).

Diversity management is not just a theoretical construct or socially desirable construct. It is gaining more popularity in the economic and business sector (Cox, 2001; Kamp & Hagedoorn-Rasmussen, 2004; Glastra et al., 2001). Businesses are beginning to feel the limits of the push towards ethnic assimilation and the negative effects of discrimination. They no longer can neglect the multi-cultural potential of the work force and clients. The Kamalo Balo example suggests that a similar change is needed in sport clubs. The incidents that involve Kamalo Balo are interpreted primarily from an integration perspective using both deficiency and discrimination frames. Instead, a fragmentation perspective could be used to explore which meanings are congruent with meanings given to ethnicity in a specific context. This requires individuals to recognize and accept differences between social positions of individuals and groups.

Many nonimmigrant sport clubs have to recognize and accept the existence of fragmentation in order to survive as a club. They must do justice to the differences and contradictions within the club that are connected with social relations such as ethnicity, gender, age and class. This recommendation applies also to immigrant clubs as well. The use of a fragmentation perspective also requires an acceptance of the complexity inherent in sense making of discrimination. When the ambiguity of social-cultural relations in organizational processes becomes a starting point for making sense of experiences however, than it may be possible to see that such experiences are layered. The saying "forget that I am black; never forget that I am black" describes this well (Applebaum, 2002). The acceptance of such ambiguities could mean that experiences (cues) such as winks, remarks, fights, and tackles could be interpreted with the use of layered meanings.

Notes

[1] This is a fictitious name.

[2] The Dutch - English dictionary (Van Dale, 1997) translates allochtoon as immigrant or foreigner and autochtoon as indigenous or native. The Central Bureau for Statistics uses the terms allochtoon and autochtoon to denote those (or their parents) who are born outside and in the Netherlands respectively (CBS, 1996). Yet, this distinction is problematic. First, the Dutch Department of Health, Welfare and Sport (VWS) creates its allochtoon policies for people whose roots are in Surinam, the Dutch Antilles, Turkey, Morocco and for those who are refugees (Elling & de Knop, 1999). People living in the Netherlands who are born in Germany, Norway or the United States for example, are not classified as allochtoon and therefore not targeted in allochtoon policies. Second, Dutch Antilleans are Dutch citizens and therefore technically cannot be classified as allochtoon that is, as foreigner or immigrant. Surinam became independent only in 1975. Those born before that date and living in the Netherlands have always had Dutch citizenship. They are not foreigners or immigrants yet are labeled as such. Possibly skin color plays a role with respect to who gets defined as allochtoon.
Making distinctions among social groups in the Netherlands is therefore fraught with difficulties. The most common labels used to designate people whose roots are in Morocco, Turkey, Dutch Antilles, Surinam and Africa are immigrant or foreigner. For lack of a better description, we have chosen to use the English translation of allochtoon and autochtoon using *immigrant* and *nonimmigrant* respectively. We realize they are fuzzy concepts.

[3] See Swank 1996; Verweel & David, 1995 for a detailed description of the study and the final report.

[4] In 1997 there were 1,435,000 people classified as immigrants living in the Netherlands. The largest groups are from Surinam (287,000), Turkey (280,000), Morocco (233,000) and the Dutch Antilles/Aruba (95,000) (SCP, 1998, pp. 241).

[5] This is also true for lesbians and gays (Elling & de Knop, 1999).

[6] Glastra et al. (1996, 2001) call this the differentiation frame and describe it as reflecting cultural complexity. We choose to use the term cultural complexity in this chapter because we define differentiation in this book in another way. Glastra et al. (2001) divide their conceptualization of a differentiation frame into 'culturalizing' and 'individualizing/ambiguity' versions that can be compared with the definitions of differentiation and fragmentation perspectives on organizing used in this book.

[7] The deficiency model is often used in sport when gender differences are iscussed. Women are seen as deficient when compared with men (Knoppers, 1992).

CHAPTER 7
"I DON'T CARE WHAT YOU PEOPLE IN HOLLAND THINK OR DO": SPORT AND INTERNATIONAL COOPERATIVE DEVELOPMENT

Jan Boessenkool & Frank van Eekeren

"These drills the Dutch coaches give us are really great. But you know, I need 25 balls for these drills and in the place we come from we only have one ball for 25 players. So what can I do? And what about these beautiful grounds and the equipment you've got in Holland? We have to share our grounds with the whole community and I only have Coca Cola bottles as cones!!! (South African participant in the Dutch Coach the Coaches program)

OVERVIEW

As the introductory chapters to this book suggest, sport plays a significant role in current processes of globalization and localization (see also Maguire, 1999). Athletes, coaches, officials and scientists sustain such processes, in part through their travel within and between nations. Experts, including those from the Netherlands, travel with increasing frequency to Third World countries to work on sport projects. One such project is the Coach the Coaches program, a joint initiative of the Dutch National Football Association (KNVB) and the South African Football Association (SAFA). Both the organizers and participants are enthusiastic about this project yet things have gone awry in a way that can best be characterized as a misfit between donor and recipient. In this chapter we explore how it is possible that what seems so straightforward at the beginning of a project can go wrong and to what extent it is related to sense making about sport and about international cooperative development.

RESEARCH QUESTION AND METHODOLOGY

What are the implications and consequences of the use of a Dutch discourse about sport and international cooperative development to implement a project in South Africa?

This case study is based on research by Van Eekeren (1997) who explored the significance of a project, 'Coach the Coaches', for various actors (organizations and individuals). The research was conducted over a period of six months in the Netherlands and in South Africa. The results were obtained through qualitative methods such as participant observation and in depth interviews. In-depth interviews were held with 50 members of the main stakeholder groups in the project: course participants, course leaders, Dutch football officials and South African football officials, representatives from Dutch governmental ministries, South African governmental ministries and sports bodies, and, sponsors. The interviews were part of an evaluation of the project and conducted when the course was completed. Participant observations were conducted during formal meetings of the stakeholders in both the Netherlands and South Africa and during initiatives in the townships. The research methodology also included an analysis of relevant printed material such as minutes of meetings, policy documents, evaluations, and, newspaper articles. We use the model of an arena, with concepts like front stage, back stage and under the stage, to illustrate various dynamics in our analysis of the implementation process of the Coach the Coaches project. The case study is analyzed through the various lenses of the perspectives of integration, differentiation and fragmentation. We end the chapter with suggestions for ways in which international cooperative development (ICD) could conduct similar projects in the future.

THE SITUATION

SPORT AND INTERNATIONAL COOPERATIVE DEVELOPMENT (ICD)

Although the globalization of sport has a relatively long history, sport has just recently come to the attention of those who work in international cooperative development (ICD) in the Netherlands. Government officials used to see sport as an unnecessary and unimportant luxury and at times, as a vestige of colonial relations (Swank & van Eekeren, 1998). Most of the attention in ICD has traditionally gone to health, agriculture, infrastructure, structural development and implementing democratic governance. Rarely was attention paid to sport. Sport, especially football, is however, part of the daily lives of millions of people in Third World countries. World Cup involvement and hype are greater in countries such as South Africa, Morocco, Nigeria, Cameroon, and Brazil than in the Netherlands. An instructor from the Dutch national football association (KNVB) who had visited Zambia and South Africa exclaimed: "I learned what is important in Africa: absolutely first is football, then eating and then sleeping and last of all, work. Football is inconceivably important there; unbelievable!" (Van Eekeren 1997, p. 49). Gradually ICD officials are beginning to grasp the significance of sport, and specifically football, in many countries. This message has already been understood by commercial or business versions of ICD. Other sectors of society are beginning to grasp the importance attached to sport in many cultures as well.[1]

Individuals and policy makers in many countries, including the Netherlands, assume that sport can play a significant role in individual development, in the improvement of health and well being, and, in enhancing societal cohesion (Pronk & Terpstra, 1998). When sport becomes part of ICD policies, however, differences in viewpoints, perceptions and objectives emerge. Those who work in ICD and in sport have the tendency to think and act according to static ideas about culture, sport, and cultural differences (Vink & Schapink,

1994; Van Eekeren, 2001). They see the sport situation in Third World countries as backward and underdeveloped and intend to help those countries to catch up. This way of thinking reflects a traditional dependency relationship between donors and recipients.

The last decades have also seen a growing interest in exploring meanings that society assigns to sport. Dutch policy makers in sport and, to a lesser degree, government officials in ICD who know relatively little about sport, tend to rely on functional perspectives when assigning meanings to sport (see for example Steenbergen & Tamboer, 1998; Steenbergen, 2004). Sport is seen as an instrument that can be used to achieve societal objectives such as personal development, integration, identification, health and well being, equity and personal satisfaction (Digel & Fornoff, 1989). Government and sport officials tend to prefer this functionalist approach, perhaps because it so easily translates into measurable objectives and methods.

Steenbergen and Tamboer (1998), two Dutch scholars in the area of sport, use a functional perspective to argue that sport has an intrinsic and an extrinsic dimension. The intrinsic dimension refers to sport participation as an end itself. Specifically, projects and programs are assumed to focus on the intrinsic aspects of sport when they are used to develop sport structures or sport skills that enable or increase participation. The extrinsic dimension refers to the use of sport to achieve societal objectives. Projects employ sport as an extrinsic instrument for example, when it is used to communicate messages about HIV/AIDS prevention. Steenbergen and Tamboer argue that the two dimensions should be kept in balance.

The categorization of sport into intrinsic and extrinsic dimensions has become the basis for a dominant Dutch functionalist discourse for looking at sport. This vision of a dichotomous nature of sport has been the central focus of the first Dutch policy document about sport and ICD and is used to justify two ICD projects Sport-Plus and Plus-Sport (Pronk en Terpstra, 1998). Sport - Plus projects emphasize intrinsic dimensions of sport while Plus-Sport projects are assumed to have an extrinsic dimension. The conceptualization of sport with the use of a dichotomous perspective seems to provide a relatively unambiguous frame for assigning meanings because it attributes specific hegemonic functions to sport. This is attractive to those whose work requires measurable and instrumental objectives. In this chapter, we will explore the results of assigning such meanings to sport and to ICDs and how they intersect in projects such as in the Coach the Coaches project in South Africa.

COACH THE COACHES PROJECT

ORIGINS

The (sport) boycott against South Africa ended when apartheid formally ended. The necessity of helping South Africa develop sport at the elite, at the township, and at the rural levels has caught the attention of the international community. Most but not all the attention has gone to elite sport. Those who have been and are negatively affected by apartheid have become a new target group for ICD. Western donors are especially active in the large townships such as Soweto and Alexandra. The goal of several projects is to keep the youth off the streets and to attain educational objectives. One such project is the Coach the Coaches project in which the KNVB (Dutch National Football Association) and SAFA (South African Football Association) worked together.

The Coach the Coaches project evolved out of another project called SCORE, which was sponsored by the Dutch government through its National Olympic Committee. A representative of this committee was in South Africa to work for SCORE when he heard that the SAFA was interested in working with the KNVB. The KNVB, the Dutch embassy in Pretoria, and, the Dutch Department of Health, Welfare, and Sport are interested and willing to pursue a cooperative project. Based on the results of pilot study conducted three years previously, the Dutch actors decide that structural and institutional cooperation between the KNVB and SAFA is desirable and that it fits the program that has been created to help black South Africa catch up. The stakeholders confirm this cooperation in a Memorandum of Understanding (1994).

The KNVB asks the Dutch Olympic Committee to make an inventory of the wishes of SAFA. Based on the results of this fact finding mission, the Dutch Olympic committee concludes that the SAFA wants Dutch assistance in setting up coaching education courses analogous to those used in the Netherlands. The subsequent grant proposal, written by the KNVB, is accepted by the Dutch Department of Health, Welfare and Sport. The objectives of the proposal are congruent with those of Plus-sport projects (extrinsic dimension of sport) because social goals take precedent over sport related objectives. Sport is considered to be the instrument to reach these goals. An increase in the number of qualified coaches will enable SAFA to offer more sport opportunities for youth; their sport participation is assumed to keep these youth off the streets and motivate them in their school work.

The Dutch agree to provide the content and arrange the practical aspects of the project. SAFA however, is less enthusiastic than the KNVB realizes. The agreement primarily mirrors what the Dutch want. SAFA recognizes the high quality of the Dutch coaching education program but does not want a carbon copy. SAFA has other interests as well. It wants to work with the KNVB at the top sport level, that is, their primary objective is to host a match between the Dutch national men's team and the South African men's team Bafana Bafana. This wish however stays unexpressed for a long time.

Since SAFA seems to have no clear wishes concerning the coaching education program, the KNVB decides to offer regular courses (clinics) in South Africa. The people from the KNVB who are involved in the project have little, if any, information about the context and situation in South Africa. In addition, no agreements or plans are made for subsequent steps beyond the holding of the clinics. The late starting date (three years after the idea is conceived) is due to problems in South Africa and, as the KNVB realizes later, to the fact that SAFA was not quite prepared for the project.

SAFA has delegated the responsibility for the organization of the project to a sponsor and a marketing firm who see commercial opportunities in the project. Suddenly there are more South African actors, each with their own interests, involved in the project. SAFA works front stage but there are others with a great deal of influence involved behind the scenes or back stage. SAFA also has trouble discerning and differentiating among the various Dutch actors and their interests. Their formal agreement is with the KNVB but the interest of and the financing by the Dutch Department of Health, Welfare and Sport play an important role. Moreover, the interests of the KNVB are not clear-cut either. Its coaching certification program has commanded international respect. The content of this coaching course selected for the Coach the Coaches project is that what is presented when it is given to Dutch coaches in the Netherlands. Obviously, the context of the project has several layers, is contextually specific and more complex than was first thought. In the following sections we trace the development of this project.

PHASE 1

White Dutch and black South African football officials, white Dutch and black South African governmental officials, and, sponsors whose representatives are white, are all involved in the project. Most of the participants in the Coach the Coaches project in South Africa are black or colored males between 20 and 40 years old. There is only one female participant who is white. Obviously, the structure and design of the project do not automatically lead to a socially demographic balance.

During the clinics, held in four different locations in South Africa, the KNVB staff and SAFA coaches meet each other for the first time. The South African coaches are surprised by the presence of the Dutch instructors. A South African coach comments that "they [the Dutch] sent two old men. We expected top coaches. They could have shown us more respect" (Van Eekeren 1997, p. 35). Moreover, the course seems to offer nothing new as the comments of a South African participant reveal: "There was not too much new that I learned there. I have had a lot of introductory courses before" (Van Eekeren 1997, p. 37).

Obviously the needs and wishes of the target group, the South African coaches, had not been considered in the planning of the project. A Dutch instructor observes: "The final goal of the project was that the coaches would instruct others, but who? Most of the participants coach children in the townships but others are schoolteachers or coach in a club. These require different approaches" (Van Eekeren 1997, p. 39).

The circumstances and facilities differ completely from when the courses are given in the Netherlands. The quotation with which we opened this chapter is a good illustration of this mismatch. South Africans live in other circumstances, in another culture, and possess skills of which the Dutch are unaware. A South African coach explains:

> We had interesting discussions with these old men. One day they were explaining to us that passing the ball with the outside of the foot wasn't right because you cannot give straight passes. So I said to them: 'Give me a ball and I show you how we do this in South Africa.' So, I gave a straight pass with the outside of my foot. They were amazed. You know our technique is far better than the Dutch!" (Van Eekeren 1997, p. 43).

Interpersonal communication was also complicated. A Dutch instructor attempts to make sense of his experiences and says: "Our [teaching] method is based on much talking and giving each other positive feedback. The South Africans were not used to this. They do not do that and respect authority. We also discovered that disagreeing with older people is not part of their culture" (Van Eekeren 1997, p. 43). Obviously, the Dutch and South African organizations involved in this project have insufficient insight into the needs and wishes of the target group.

PHASE 2

The management and council of SAFA show little interest in the grassroots project, that is, in the clinics. "SAFA only believes in Bafana Bafana [national team]. They do not believe in development. They are not interested in our problems. That is why they do not support us with finances or equipment, not even with words!" says a coach from Durban (van Eekeren, 1997, p. 37). Another South African coach speaks for many when he says: "SAFA needs the sponsor's money and the sponsor uses the coaches, the KNVB, for their advertising campaign and us! They come only to impress the public" (Van Eekeren 1997, p. 37). In short, they suspect that only the objectives of the Dutch and the interests of the South African sponsors play a role in the setting up and holding of the courses. Differences between and within organizations and SAFA's lack of clarity about its needs, contribute to this perception. Not all the stakeholders are aware that the process creates differences and multiple layers.

The project continues. Representatives of the KNVB come to South Africa to discuss the continuation of the project with the sponsors and the marketing firm. When the KNVB people arrive in Johannesburg, they discover that a sponsor has already printed and distributed glossy brochures containing an overview of the program for the coming month and emphasizing the contribution of the KNVB while the role of SAFA is minimized. The KNVB knows nothing about this. According to the brochures, the KNVB will educate several national coaches who subsequently will conduct courses at the grass roots level. SAFA invites 40 coaches to attend a continuation course in Johannesburg. Nine coaches will be selected from this group to attend a two-week course at KNVB headquarters in the Netherlands. This selection process is not straightforward, however.

The interpersonal histories, concerns, emotions and, other issues continually play an important role in the ways in which the project develops. The region north of Johannesburg, for example, is not represented in the continuation course. Several people say that this absence is due to a disagreement between a coach instructor and a SAFA official. In addition, another coaching course, organized by another sponsor of SAFA, is held simultaneously in the same complex and is labeled by the SAFA representative as "the real SAFA course; they are the real coaches of South Africa" (Van Eekeren 1997, p. 37). Obviously there is a great struggle among commercial interests for the product "football".

The competition among the 40 South African coaches for the nine tickets to the Netherlands increases the mutual mistrust. An instructor from the KNVB says: "Those coaches were afraid that the people from SAFA would select other coaches behind closed doors" (Van Eekeren 1997, p. 51). Emotions of and interpersonal relationships among the actors surface and shed new light on the context and on the processes of sense making. To many coaches it becomes clear that a lot is going on back stage and under the stage. Decisions are not based on what is happening front stage only. The coaches gradually understand that they have to influence the processes back stage and under stage to make certain they will be selected. Eventually nine coach-instructors are selected.

The selected coach-instructors come to the Netherlands and have an opportunity to take in all the dimensions of football in the Netherlands. The KNVB allows them to look behind the scenes as well. This results in some dissatisfaction among the visiting coaches as they realize that several things need to be changed at the organizational level in football in South Africa. A coach-instructor says: "It is sad to realize that in South Africa there is no structure! I am telling you: our national office cannot compare to one of your district offices. Our time in Holland made clear that we have to work hard" (Van Eekeren, 1997, p. 59). Neither the SAFA nor the sponsors welcome these types of critical comments about organizational structure.

They feel that the coach instructors should confine their comments to football. They say: "We are not in Holland, we are not the KNVB!!" (Van Eekeren 1997, p. 59). Obviously, the content of the Dutch program is not automatically congruent with the South African context. The various South African actors assign different meanings to the content of the project. A South African coach-instructor sighs: "Sometimes we had to realize that we were in Holland to learn and share ideas, not to change" (Van Eekeren 1997, p. 61).

The KNVB assumes it has built up much credit with the SAFA after the four clinics, the continuation/selection course in Johannesburg, and, the two-week course in the Netherlands. Yet, these efforts by the KNVB do not mean that the SAFA automatically prefers to work with them. The SAFA chooses a German coach, for example, to be the director of coaches while the KNVB had expected to appoint a Dutch coach to fill the position. The relationship between the KNVB and SAFA becomes guarded after this. Yet, the Dutch and South African national teams do play a friendly match in Johannesburg in June 1997. The occurrence of this match means that SAFA has achieved one of its most important objectives.

The KNVB admits that it understands little of the way SAFA operates. Cultural differences are cited as a possible reason for this. Other explanations are possible as well. Perhaps the motivation to work together was minimal or lacking. Or possibly the individuals from SAFA have ways of sense making that the Dutch failed to recognize because they were different from their own.
Also, the Dutch may have based their reasoning on dominant Dutch assumptions about culture and about the nature of sport. Possibly too, SAFA is a smart recipient that exactly knows what the donor wants to hear or read. In the following sections we explore the process of development of the Coach the Coaches project to gain some clarity about what went wrong to gain insight into the processes and to raise awareness of roles various actors play in this project.

MULTIPLE LAYERS IN THE ARENA

The Coach the Coaches project can be seen as a multi-layered arena. There is no agreement on what is the relevant front stage of the coaching program. Back stage stakeholders negotiate or even fight to realize their interests. Relationships among the stakeholders (under the stage) prove to have great influence on the processes that occur front stage and back stage. The project suggests that the arena of the Coach the Coaches project is larger, has more layers, and is more complex than originally thought by KNVB and SAFA. Consequently, it is not surprising that activities are not coordinated with each other.

SENSE MAKING

The sense making of Dutch sport officials and government officials dominate the project Their own experiences and the dominant discourses about sport and ICD in the Netherlands serve as their frame and become embedded in the project. Discussions about the project take place primarily within their own networks and exclude the recipients. There has been little, if any, acknowledgment of interpersonal, cultural, historical, and situational differences. This neglect of interpersonal and cross-cultural differences means that expectations for the project are also diverse. As the time to start of the project approached and the contacts with the South African actors grew, the diversity in expectations became clearer and some adjustments were made, primarily through trial and error. Yet, because the sense making of the South African coaches remained subordinate to those of the Dutch, the results of the project became less than expected.

There were many questions, such as: Why did the Dutch actors not implement the information and knowledge gained through their interactions with South Africans? Why did the South African participants not clarify their expectations and wishes for the project? Is this a result of an uncritical use of a functionalist perspective of sport as described earlier in this chapter? In other words, do both the South African and Dutch participants assume that sport participation has primarily positive outcomes for all those involved? Is the relationship between the dominant discourses used by the Dutch and possibly alternate discourses of the South Africans a result of the complexity of intercultural management? In what manner is this complexity enhanced by interpersonal interactions and relationships and by cultural differences, historical colonial relationships, interests, and emotions? Specifically, to what extent is every actor a prisoner of her or his own context?

INTEGRATION PERSPECTIVE

The Dutch often describe the mission of ICD as a search for bridges across cultural gaps (van Eekeren, 1997). This idea suggests that the meanings assigned by the donor and the recipient are equally important. The results of this study suggest however, that activities of ICD often reinforce the status quo as seen through the eyes of the donor country. The one-way-is best strategy seems to dominate ICD and is exemplified by the KNVB's decision to offer its successful Dutch coaching courses in South Africa. This ignores the specific situation in South Africa. Possibly sport officials and those in ICD assume that globalization has led to a standardization and uniformity within the world of football and that this enables them to offer a Dutch course in South Africa without making any adjustment or changes. This vision is often described as McDonaldization and assumes a trend or movement toward cultural convergence or growing sameness (Hannerz, 1992). It represents the classical vision of modernization as a steam roller that denies and eliminates cultural differences that get in its way. MacDonaldization simultaneously represents the theme of modernization and the theme of cultural imperialism and is congruent with an integration perspective.

Policy making by donors, it seems, is sensitive to trends, especially to those in its own country. The key objectives of ICD in the Netherlands continually change. Recipient countries have grown accustomed to this and primarily try to survive. Their dependency on grants may push them to implement policies of donor countries. Representatives of target groups in ICD have become professional and smart/strategic recipients who know exactly what donors want to hear and see in a grant proposal. Consequently there may be little room, if any, for perspectives and values of recipients.

DIFFERENTIATION PERSPECTIVE

Although the desires and needs of the recipients are not incorporated into the Coach the Coaches project, the Dutch attribute the problems that emerge during the course of the project to the fact that SAFA is different. A differentiation approach to organizations, globalization and ICD emphasizes cultural differences among various groups (Nederveen Pieterse, 1996:1389; Verweel, Chapter 2). Failure to recognize cultural differences between the Netherlands and South Africa may in part be responsible for the decision of the KNVB to give its own courses in four South African cities. In addition, the relationship between the SAFA and KNVB could also be characterized by a dependency of the smart recipient (SAFA and South African coaches) on the donor (Dutch Department of Health, Welfare and Sport and KNVB) who tries to sell its own perspective on football. As is evident in the foregoing, the various actors involved in the Coach the Coaches project do not always understand each other. The discussions between the KNVB and SAFA, for example, do not always go as the Dutch expect. Thus, a differentiation perspective may partially explain the limited success of the project. Yet the Dutch actors do use the differentiation perspective but do so primarily in an undifferentiated way ignoring other forms of differentiation.

First, referring to "the" South African culture or to typical cultural aspects of the KNVB is a simplification of reality. South African culture is as heterogeneous as is the culture within the Netherlands. In addition, the data show that organizational cultural differences between the KNVB and the Dutch Department of Health, Welfare and Sport also result in an initial lack of clarity about the project. Heterogeneity also typifies the organizational cultures of SAFA and KNVB themselves. Even within a relatively small organization as the KNVB cultural differences exist, for example between coaches and staff members or between younger and older employees. Similarly organizational cultural differences between the headquarters and the regional offices of SAFA also play a role in this project. The context differs not only for the different organizations involved in the project but also for the different staff members *within* the organizations.

Secondly, the explanatory power of an undifferentiated cultural difference approach ignores both the individual and the context. Interactions between individuals and members of organizations are not only influenced by their cultural backgrounds but also by relationships of power, by meanings given to social group relations such as race and ethnicity, and by personal interests, interpersonal rivalries and emotions.

Third, the explanatory power of cultural differences for all that goes wrong with the project is also limited because it defines culture in a narrow integrative way. There is for example, little evidence that the notion of cultural difference as claimed by the Dutch actors includes a recognition of issues of social diversity.

Obviously then, other forms of differentiation occur in addition to inter-country cultural differences. The immediate reaction when an ICD project does not work out as expected however is to blame the other culture and to work within a framework of stereotypes about that culture. This reaction is a common occurrence in organizations that are confronted with noticeable cultural differences (Peters & Waterman, 1982; Deal & Kennedy, 1982; Hofstede, 1992). Proponents of an undifferentiated differentiation perspective tend to see differences as unproductive, as being short term and changeable, and, primarily as a source of unwelcome rivalry and conflict. Since differences occur that cannot be integrated into the dominant framework for sense making, they acknowledge those differences and see them as contributing to the failure of the project.

Van Eekeren, (1997) concludes that the Dutch individuals and their organizations who were involved in the Coach the Coaches project had the tendency to reason in an unproblematic and homogeneous way using their own context as starting point. The use of an integration perspective seemed to dominate their thinking while they simultaneously used a narrow version of a differentiation perspective to explain existing differences.

HYBRIDIZATION OR FRAGMENTATION PERSPECTIVE

Another perspective, hybridization, could have been used however, that might have dissolved the oppositional nature of the two perspectives (Hannerz 1992; Latour 1994; Parker 2000; Martin 2002). It emphasizes the idea that global powers are and will always be quite vulnerable to very small scale and local resistance.

Hybridization acknowledges that communities as well as the people engaged in them, are always in a state of flux and divided; "groups and individuals are perpetually escaping communities as well as mobilizing to enforce them" (Kalb, 1997, P. 240). This hybridization perspective is closely aligned with the fragmentation perspective (see also Verweel & Anthonissen, Chapter 6 on this point). It sees the construction of meaning as a socio-cultural process. Blommaert (1995) says:

I have never seen cultures communicating with each other, confronting each other or having a conflict with each other. I have however seen contacts and conflicts between individuals and institutions, each time within a specific historical, social, cultural, political and situational context but never as ideal carriers of an objectively defined culture" (p. 9).

We argue that analyses of processes of sense making that occurs through interactions between individuals, organizations and cultures require a contextual hybrid approach.

SENSE MAKING ABOUT SPORT AND ICD

This case study yields several insights about meanings given to sport and ICD. The Dutch Department of Health, Welfare and Sport underwrites this Plus-Sport project because it assumes that societal objectives such as individual development and well being can be partially realized through sport projects (Pronk en Terpstra, 1998). The data show that these objectives however, are not necessarily congruent with the goals the coaches have for this project. The organizations that carry out the project, such as the sponsors, KNVB and SAFA, agree to these objectives in principle but seem to work primarily on furthering their own interests. The printing of the glossy brochures by the sponsor gives the KNVB little playing room. Dutch courses are used in the project with the assumption that their content will help the South African coaches reach the stated objectives of a Dutch governmental agency. Their initial assumption that this project has primarily extrinsic dimensions may have given Dutch officials tunnel vision so that the wishes and concerns of SAFA are not heard.

These different interests suggest that seeing sport only as a dichotomous practice can be problematic and ignores the complexity of meanings given to sport. What is intrinsic to one actor at one point of time may be extrinsic at another time. Similarly, while policy makers use sport as a tool to reach social objectives, the participants themselves give it different meanings. Those who take part in sport may not see it as an instrument for social development. They may dream about becoming famous soccer players and/or play primarily because they like it! The meanings that the South African coaches assign to the Coach the Coaches project differ from those assigned by Dutch coaches to the same courses. Some South African coaches see the course as an ideal way to spend their time: "I want to live football every minute of my life!!" (Van Eekeren 1997, p. 37) and as part of their own skill development. Others view the course as part of a commitment to their community: "I had the opportunities that other people in my community didn't have" (Van Eekeren 1997, p. 40).

In addition, the meanings assigned to football in South Africa as THE sport for blacks and coloreds are quite different from those given to it in the Netherlands. As a South African coach said: "You know to be honest, I don't care what you people in Holland think or do. I live here in this mess, but as long as I can play football it's all right!" (Van Eekeren, 1997, p. 40). The use of instrumental /functional ideas about sport and ICD in current policy seems to create a situation in which the needs and wishes of the target group can easily fade into the background.

The use of a dichotomous perspective for assigning meanings to sport may have created a frame for sense making that could not incorporate ambiguities or complexities. Reaching agreement on meanings assigned to sport may be impossible since meanings are always dependent on both actors and context. The definitions of the Dutch actors not only dominated the Coach the Coaches project but also changed over time. Attempts to create a permanent definition of sport for everyone that will still count for tomorrow and the day after tomorrow reflect a static and normative approach. The results of the Coach the Coaches project show that flexibility in coping with ever changing circumstances may be a key factor to success of a project. This flexibility is antithetical to a perspective that sees sport as having a permanent dichotomous nature.

A focus on sport as instrument as is done in Plus-Sport projects may also mean that most of the attention is given to achieving societal objectives based on the perceptions of the donor who in this case were Dutch officials. The assignment of meanings by the recipients, the coaches in the townships, may become secondary as it did in this case study. The analysis shows that giving instruction to coaches to enable children in the townships to play football in organized competition does not ensure that this will stimulate the development of these children beyond their ability to play football. Nor is there evidence of an increase in cohesion within the township. In other words, the meanings assigned to the project are dependent on meanings assigned to sport (and ICD) by the various organizations and actors involved with the project and the interaction processes among them. Obviously sport cannot be defined without involving the actors and the context in which it takes place. Giving meanings to sport therefore, is a fluid process of sense making than of static categorization. This fluidity is congruent with a hybrid or fragmentation perspective

DISCUSSION AND CONCLUSION

The actual activities of the project Coach the Coaches are the result of interactions/ discussions between the various actors and the meanings they assign to the various situations, to sport, to relationships and to ICD. The case study illustrates how existing relationships are reproduced in daily interactions and how cultural and communication differences receive their meaning within the context of the relational aspects of ICD. The age of the coaches sent by the Dutch to South Africa is not a problem in itself. In fact, South Africans might appreciate being instructed by such respected men. The previous history of this project ensures however that the presence of the old men taps into another reaction.

Actors intentionally and unintentionally draw upon the power associated with their status and their social group memberships in specific contexts. They use this to create norms, definitions and to give meanings to emotions within a context. The context is complex because it is layered, multidimensional and contextually specific. This complexity is apparent in the Coach the Coaches project. The focal points are the interactions among individuals who are influenced by their context. Discussions between the head of education programs of the KNVB and the chair of the SAFA for example, occur in a multi-layered context because the course of each discussion is influenced by the time, place, previous discussions, latest developments in the general and job context, topic, interests, emotions, etc. The general context of the donor's country, not the recipient, tends to be the most relevant determinant in the donor's course of action. Government (and football) officials seem to be more intent on pleasing their superiors than the recipient. Although the KNVB has honorable intentions in offering assistance to South Africa, it also needs a good working relationship with the Dutch Department of Health, Welfare and Sport because the government is a major grant giver to sport and creates rules and regulations that affect football. The same can be said for the SAFA.

It needs its sponsors more than it needs to have a strong relationship with Dutch organizations. The agency of the actors involved in this study can therefore, best be described as interdependent, shaped by the worlds they live and work in and in which decisions are based, in part, on strategies that compare the different needs and interests with each other.

The foregoing may make it seem that actors are prisoners of their context. This is not totally true. The place, the nature of the walls and the design of the prison can be altered. Systems can change when relations among actors and structure change (Giddens, 1979; 1984). Actor and structure are in a dialectical, not oppositional, relationship. As Verweel (Chapter 2) argues, reality is created by social constructions that flow from the ways actors make sense of situations.

These constructions can be contradictory and often ambiguous; they require the lens of a fragmentation perspective to be seen as such. The dialectical relationship between agency and structure gives actors room for implementing structural change. Current relationships may be deeply rooted but they are produced and reproduced by all those involved. Actors can exert influence on current relationships especially in a new policy area such as sport and ICD. Sport organizations and ICD organizations are relatively new partners; this newness enables them to establish an original relationship within the structure of ICD. These relationships can possibly be developed in interactions with each other and with partners on the other side of the world.

Effecting change also requires insight into the structural relationships and the context of the actors who are involved (Giddens, 1979; 1984). Historical relationships between the Netherlands and South Africa and contextual meanings given to sport play a role in joint projects. Relationships of dependency and power are difficult to change but insight into personal situationality and the arena in which one is acting is crucial. This arena and its context are constantly changing, and are dynamic. A raised consciousness is not just confined to an examination of the situation and self but is an ongoing process in which learning and doing are inextricably linked.

The use of a fragmentation perspective has consequences for those who make and for those who implement policy (Martin 2002). A fragmentation perspective assigns agency to everyone who is involved with the writing and implementation of policy and assumes that every action has meaning and that those meanings are fluid. The use of a fragmentation perspective implies that objectives for an ICD sport project cannot be established ahead of time or be described in precise terms since the process is a dynamic one.

Those who create policy need to keep in mind the reasons for the project without requiring concrete measurable results in terms of donor's wishes. Those who implement policies need to be very sensitive to the contributions of others, to be reflective about the role played social relations, and, be very flexible in their work. Both groups need to give a project room to develop and take its course. This approach means that the usual methods used to evaluate ICD projects may not be suitable because they tend to fix the course and content of the project. The use of monitoring during the project may be more suitable than the measuring of results at the end. The creation and implementation of policies and joint projects therefore, require reflexivity and flexibility with respect to differences and ambiguities in sense making, to formulating goals, and to the actual content and conduct of activities.

Notes

[1] This was evident in the interest shown in the symposium about sport and ICD. The Center for Policy and Management of the University of Utrecht in cooperation with the Department of Foreign Affairs and the Department of Health, Welfare and Sport, organized a symposium "Sport and international development," on January 16, 1998. More than 100 representatives from sport, ICD, the government and higher education attended. Those who attended showed interest in the role sport plays in African society. The government, represented by former government leaders Terpstra and Pronk, built on this interest to develop the first Dutch governmental policy statement about this subject entitled: "Sport and development: Team work scores!" (Pronk & Terpstra, 1998). In November 2003 "The Next Step", an expert meeting of officials and administrators involved in sport, was held in the Netherlands and attended by more than 100 participants from all over the world.

CHAPTER 8
ORGANIZING VIEWPOINT DIVERSITY AND/OR ORGANIZING SOCIAL DIVERSITY?

Annelies Knoppers and Anton Anthonissen

OVERVIEW

The introductory chapters of this book emphasize that sport and the rest of society continue to be subjected to changes that constantly require shifts in sense making about diversity and cohesion. Sport associations and in particular, their boards of directors, must deal with this increase in diversity in sense making and erosion of community loyalty and ties. The first two chapters of this book describe theoretical insights about processes of sense making and how individuals use it to assign meanings to experiences and to social differences in and outside sport. Sport administrators and officials shape the dominant ways or frames through which events or cues are viewed and assigned meanings within their sport clubs. The various case studies discussed in this book illustrate interpretive processes that those in leadership positions in sport organizations use to deal with many issues that often accompany and require individual and organizational change. Sport administrators, officials and athletes constantly rearrange existing and new 'facts' to fit them into a specific frame. These arrangements always have consequences for sport organizations and for organizational members. In this closing chapter, we discuss the commonalities and disparities of the findings in the various case studies and place those findings in a broader perspective that connects and contextualizes the two ways of sense making of diversity.

COMMONALITIES ACROSS CASE STUDIES

Although each has a different theme, the five case studies have at least two commonalities. One commonality is the similarity in meanings given to sport and the role these meanings play in shaping viewpoints and social relations.

MEANINGS GIVEN TO SPORT

The sport administrators and officials involved in these case studies tend to direct most of their energy and attention to elite sport. In the case studies about professionalization and about mergers, board members use a desired improvement of the first men's team to persuade athletes, other club members, and, important stakeholders to agree with their plans for the future of the club. This preference for elite sport is not unique to Dutch sport. The discourse that positions elite performance as a main attribute of sport also dominates global societal discourses about competitive sport. The South Africa Football Association (SAFA) for example, wants to improve the competencies of its coaches through coaching education courses but more important, wants its national men's team to play the Dutch team (see Chapter 7). Elite sport or high level performance tends to be globally framed as the most important and most interesting level of competition, as a potential source of income, as a tool that can be used to enhance social integration, and, as a vehicle to foster local, national and international pride (Coakley, 2004; Kearney, 1992; Knoppers & Anthonissen, 2001). A team, especially a men's team, that plays at the elite level is assumed to work as a magnet for sponsors, athletes and spectators, to increase the popularity of a sport, and/or, to contribute to social cohesion and local or national visibility. This global discursive practice strengthens the association between elite sport and young men (Messner, 1992; 2002). The performance and behaviors of elite male athletes tend to be used to create the norm by which other teams and/or athletes are judged. Consequently, they provide a norm for differentiation as the case study about coaching indicated. This preference for elite sport is therefore not just contextually confined to the Dutch setting but part of the globalization of sport. This preference for elite sport by administrators and officials is not the only commonality across all the case studies, however.

PREFERENCE FOR HOMOGENEITY IN SENSE MAKING

In each of these case studies, sport administrators show a strong preference for homogeneity in viewpoints. This preference becomes a driving force behind their actions. Although many acknowledge the existence of differences in the assignment of meanings within their sport clubs or organizations, sport administrators tend to interpret those differences negatively and act in various ways to obtain consent for their frames and to minimize or marginalize differences. The case study that focuses on a dominant discursive shift to professionalization, for example, shows how board members try to obtain consent for a change in organizational emphasis. These board members seem to assume that the club is unified prior to this shift and subsequently, do all they can to persuade everyone that a shift to professionalization is the best and only way for the club to survive. They make every effort to obtain consent for their frames despite resistance.

In contrast to an initial assumption of unity, sport administrators in several other case studies acknowledge differences at the outset. Although coaches and board members implicitly admit that sport clubs have historically been male bastions for example, they try to deal with changes in the gender make up of sport clubs by creating and reinforcing discourses emphasizing meritocracy and neutrality that seem to eradicate such differences. Every attempt is made to create and strengthen discourses that reduce social differences based on gender. Similarly, the merger of two clubs is based on the initial premise that each club has different strengths and weaknesses. A merger is assumed to eliminate acknowledged weaknesses. The creation of a new club and the processes of assigning meanings to it, however, include attempts by board members to erase or minimize differences in history, culture and purpose. This erasure ultimately results in a loss of members and of volunteers. The merged club is less than the sum of its two clubs. The same acknowledgement of initial difference occurs in the case study involving the Netherlands and South Africa. The actors involved in the Coach the Coaches project know that the two countries are different but seem to assume that meanings given to sport are globalized so that a course created for the Netherlands can also be given successfully in South Africa. Differences that become visible once the project is underway tend to be seen as inevitable and attributed to cultural differences, that is, to ways South Africans and Dutch people may differ in their habits, ways of interacting and preferences. This assumption of initial difference also occurs in the Kamalo Balo case study, although in more subtle ways. Those involved in that case study seem to be aware that the clubs have different backgrounds but appear to assume that playing competitive football negates those differences while at the same time, they attribute many behaviors that occur before, during or after competitions to ethnic differences.

Obviously then, the sport administrators and officials in all these case studies expend a great deal of energy to achieve integration or consent for change although differences and ambiguities are present. They ignore or minimize these complexities in sense making at great cost to their organization or project. This result confirms McPhee & Zaug's (2001) argument that organizational members "with sufficient commitment and resources can get things accomplished but rarely as much as they intended or with the outcomes they imagined" (p. 585).

This minimization of differences is not just confined to Dutch sport, however, but reflects the dominant culture of Western sport organizations (Doherty & Chelladurai, 1999). The values and assumptions of the dominant group tend to be adopted by members of such organizations. It is not surprising then, that when sport administrators do experience differentiation; they use various overlapping strategies to establish *their* frame or discourse as the dominant discourse and to achieve consent for it.

Stategies to Obtain Consent

Persuasion

The board members featured in these case studies tend to rely on their persuasive powers and skills to obtain support for their ways of framing and reacting to issues. Club members/athletes who were part of the merger and professionalization case studies are promised a stronger club if they agree to the proposed changes. Similarly, nonimmigrants collectively use stereotypes to persuade each other and themselves that competing against an immigrant club is dangerous. Also, coaches and board members use a discourse of meritocracy and of normative maleness to persuade others and themselves that the under-representation of women coaches is not the fault of a club or sport organization. Persuasion is obviously a popular strategy. Perhaps the choice for this strategy is not surprising since club members are volunteers. If members are not persuaded of the advantages of a proposal they may vote it down at a membership meeting, join another club, quit the sport, get involved in another sport, and/or, practice the sport in an informal setting. In this way voluntary organizations are different from nonvoluntary ones such as work organizations. Work organizations select and chose their members while the reverse is true for voluntary organizations: athletes chose or create a club and ask board members to administer it for them! Thus it is not surprising that persuasion is a commonly used strategy. Although persuasion is a dominant strategy, it is not the only one used to obtain consent, however.

APPEALS TO SELF INTEREST

Appeals to self-interest are also used to obtain consent. South African coaches attend the clinics and courses not necessarily because they support the dominant Dutch discourses about sport but more important, because they love football and/or because there is a chance of 'winning' a trip to the Netherlands. Several players in the Third Half (Verweel, Chapter 2) appeal to the other players to continue with the team so that they can continue to play in their current division. Self interest is transformed into a collective interest. Members of sport clubs featured in these case studies tend to accept changes as long as their own interests and the meanings they assign to club membership are protected.

SUPPORT OF STAKEHOLDERS

Another way of finding support for a viewpoint is to form coalitions, especially with important stakeholders, who hold similar beliefs. The various case studies show how colleagues at other sport clubs affirm viewpoints of board members. Grant giving agencies, sponsors, the media, local and national government officials, and, administrators from national sport organizations take on the role of stakeholder and often support the dominant discourses as well. These colleagues and stakeholders also tend to represent the same social position held by most of the board members in sport clubs, that is, they tend to be white heterosexual males associated with a certain type of masculinity. Yet, even here differentiation occurs. Board members and stakeholders who are similarly positioned socially do not always agree with each other; battles are fought back stage to ensure that a certain discourse becomes dominant (see for example, Anthonissen, Chapter 3).

IGNORE OR MARGINALIZE DIFFERENCES

Sometimes sport administrators use coercion and/or ignore or marginalize alternate discourses to attain consent. Synergus is chosen as name for the new club after the merger of Bunder and Donaro although members vote against the name. Similarly, the use of the performance of outstanding male performers as the norm, means that men and women coaches can minimize and neutralize gendered culture and access to resources. Likewise, many members of PTP do not want to see their club professionalized in such a way that a majority of its energies and resources flow toward the top men's team. Many of the athletes believe their competition and team is as important as that of the first men's team; their discourse, which prioritizes self-improvement and enjoyment in meanings assigned to competition, is ignored and coopted. Board members circumvent the concerns of these members by creating a foundation and a business club. Satisfying these sponsors/ stakeholders is perceived to be more important than attending to the different meanings club members assign to their membership. At the same time, this complicity of board members with external stakeholders is framed as meeting the needs and interests of athletes whose membership fees will not be increased. Obviously then, board members involved in these case studies acknowledge differences but do not want those differences to make a difference.

USE OF MARKET DISCOURSE

Sport administrators also use market forces to gain consent while those forces simultaneously also shape the actions of the administrators. The ways in which market discourses are used and play a role in various case studies are illustrative of sport as a half-open system. The KNVB and SAFA for example, use grants (for the development of South African football coaches) to safeguard and augment their own position in various ways. The KNVB reinforces its role as the developer of coaching education courses and the SAFA uses the project to attract sponsors. Both try to satisfy the demands of grant givers. Similarly, board members involved in the merger and the professionalization case studies want to use current market forces to professionalize their clubs. They (re) produce a discourse that links the performance level of the first men's team to an increase in participatory opportunities for all athletes although this means that the first men's team receives the most attention, resources and publicity. As stated earlier, a dominant discourse about the pyramidal structure assumes that the better the first men's team performs and therefore entertains, the greater the number of athletes who will be attracted to the club and possibly join it. Thus market forces are assigned a predominant role in the discourses used by board members to persuade club members that they should accept the current situation or the results of change.

USE OF CULTURAL DIFFERENCES

Obviously, sport administrators and officials do everything they can to gain consent and to minimize and marginalize differences. At the same time however, they do not completely ignore differences. There are occasions when they construct differences to explain events. The case study about sport and international development focuses on differences in meanings that participants from two different countries assign to a cooperative project. The participants ground their explanation of what went wrong in cultural differences. The use of cultural differences to justify unexpected results also occurs in the creation of frames to explain incidents involving Kamalo Balo and other clubs.

The incidents of violence in matches involving only nonimmigrants as well as the social diversity of nonimmigrant clubs are ignored as nonimmigrants create a cultural difference frame to assign meanings to events involving Kamalo Balo. By creating Kamalo Balo as different, they are able to blame its members for a violent incident at a football match. Immigrant athletes also use a contextual frame but in a different way. As Verweel and Knoppers (Chapter 1) show, meanings are continually being (re) produced as actors try to make sense of the "what, why and who" in their different worlds. These worlds include their participation in sport, their tasks as board members in sport organizations, their role as sport fans, their home life, and, their responsibilities at home and in paid labor and in the community. Thus, members of Kamalo Balo use their experiences of being discriminated against in the work force to assume that they will experience discrimination in sport. Sense making based on cultural differences can therefore be used to explain what goes wrong.

RESISTANCE

Athletes or club members seem to have little voice in the decision-making processes in these case studies. Board members require athletes, other officials, and those in leadership positions such as coaches, to accept and use the prevailing or changing discourses. This does not mean that athletes are passive victims however; they use their power in various ways: by distancing themselves from their clubs, by silence, by grumbling/ dissenting, by not attending general meetings, by guarding their own interests, and/or, by dropping out. Women athletes may not even attempt to become a coach or have the ambition to coach an elite team (Knoppers & Bouman, 1996; 1998).

Women coaches may perceive they are not welcome and leave the club or the coaching profession. Board and club members who disagree tend to leave the club or resign from their position. Some athletes establish their own clubs like those at Kamalo Balo did. Obviously, efforts by administrators to achieve consent at all costs can result in unacknowledged differentiation and in a loss of membership and of motivation to volunteer for activities. Every attempt seems to be made to erase acknowledged differences in viewpoints and in social diversity. This erasure typifies the dominant way in which sport administrators and officials in these case studies operate.

DIVERSITY IN VIEWPOINTS AND SOCIAL DIVERSITY

Although board members try to ignore differentiation, differences in viewpoints and in social groups are present in all the case studies. While the focus in some of the studies is on differences in viewpoints, social forces such as gender and ethnicity are also present. Similarly in the case studies that focus on aspects of social diversity, differentiation also occurs within categorical group membership. Thus in essence, all of the case studies involve both types of diversity; in fact, the two types of diversity overlap.

VIEWPOINT DIVERSITY

In four case studies, differences are defined primarily in terms of viewpoints; little reference is made to social differences or to the social group membership of the key actors in these case studies. Specifically, differences in sense making are not attributed to race or gender or other social relations such as age, and sexual preference. Board members of nonimmigrant sport clubs and leaders of the KNVB do not connect their own ways of sense making, of shifting discourses, and of forcing integration, to their ways of enacting a certain type of white heterosexual masculinity.

Social group membership and accompanying status and positioning are not constructed as issues and are made invisible. Consequently, these sport administrators and officials are able to sustain the power that accompanies their positions and their unacknowledged societal privileges. This enables them to create the dominant frames that club members must use to make sense of the situation.

SOCIAL DIVERSITY

In contrast to a focus on diversity of viewpoints, meanings given to social relations are the explicit focus in the case studies about gender and about ethnicity. Board members in these case studies are confronted with differentiation among individuals but deal with it in ways similar to those used by sport administrators when faced with viewpoint diversity. Their emphasis on integration means that patterns of social group discrimination are not recognized. In addition, differences between social groups and in social power are not taken seriously or rarely acknowledged since everyone is assumed to have equal opportunity to participate in sport (Prasad, 1997; Knoppers, Chapter 5). Although differences in meanings assigned to masculinity and femininity become visible when women enter the predominantly male coaching ranks, meritocratic and male normative discourses are used to neutralize this entry. In addition, when board members do react to gender and ethnic issues, they see their own reactions as unrelated to the social positioning that accompanies their own gender and ethnic identities. The images and behaviors of the 'other' are framed as the central dimension of sense making of social diversity. Board members seem to reflect little on their own multiple identities and the privileges that accompany them. They tend to see performance/behavior as the sole responsibility of the 'other'. The social context and support systems, or lack there of for women and ethnic minorities, are totally ignored and/or receive little attention. This means that differences in viewpoints are visible but not attributed to individuals, as occurs in the other case studies, but are assigned in a one-dimensional manner to social group membership.

This unidimensionality in categorization can be problematic. For example, the coaches described by Knoppers (Chapter 5) define gender primarily in a categorical way. Consequently, the issue of the under-representation of women and over-representation of men is framed as a problem owned by women and not as a problem of definitions given to masculinity or to white ethnicity. Similarly, the actors involved in the case study about Kamalo Balo frame events in terms of ethnicity but not of gender although all the participants are males. Interestingly, the participants in the Coach the Coaches project focus more on assumed national characteristics than on ethnicity in explaining what went wrong. If the case study had focused on a cooperative project between Dutch and French football associations in which relatively few of the original objectives had also been realized, that lack of success might also have been attributed to cultural differences. When Dutch officials use only cultural differences to explain the difficulties in the progress of the cooperative project with South Africa, then status differences remain unnamed. The participants in this project pay little attention to the ways that interactions among the various actors and the ways in which the project develops are influenced by meanings given to skin color, to historical dynamics as colonizer/colonized, and, to gender. The issues and problems in these three case studies are not attributed to social constructions or to ways in which sense is made of a situation. Specifically, social relations are constructed primarily as categories that create difference and not as forces that are embedded in identifications and interactions.

THREE PERSPECTIVES FOR DEALING WITH DIVERSITY

INTEGRATION

The results of the case studies make it obvious that not only do these sport administrators have an overwhelming preference for an integration perspective but also that the sole use of this perspective can have negative outcomes. Board members are well intentioned and are not naïve, however. Why then do they have this strong preference for an integration perspective? A number of explanations may account for this preference. First, the preference for an integration perspective is not just confined to the sport setting. Research on organizations in sport and nonsport settings has shown that although viewpoint and social diversity are valued in organizational rhetoric, social practices are predominantly grounded in integration perspectives (Bissett, 2004; Martin, 1992). Second, the nature of the results may be due in part to the retrospective nature of sense making (Isabella, 1990; Weick, 1995). These analyses were all made a posteriori. An analysis that incorporates the benefit of hindsight may provide a more holistic view than one that is conducted during a process.

Third, this preference for and use of the integration perspective may also be part of an attempt by sport administrators to manage uncertainty (Reynolds & Trehan, 2003). Managers in nonsport organizations also often use integration perspectives when uncertainty is seen as something to be controlled and managed. Much of the management literature and popular management books focus on managing and resolving difference (Kirby & Harter, 2003). This literature teaches administrators and managers that organizational members must develop and embrace a shared pattern of standards and values so that the organization can function efficiently. This use of the integration perspective as a reaction to uncertainty and is therefore, not specific to the Dutch context or to sport. This literature that recommends the integration perspective is part of a classical sociological paradigm, often called functionalism.[1]

Functionalists assume that society functions adequately only when there is a consensus about fundamental values and norms among the various groups in society. It is assumed that diversity, that is, a lack of like-mindedness, will cause a society to disintegrate. As we show further on, sport is assumed to play an important role in combating this disintegration. The emphasis on integration by sport administrators is therefore, not unexpected.

This integrative or functionalist perspective is not just dominant in the sport world but also provides a theoretical basis for what has been called 'corporate culture' (see for example Peters & Waterman, 1982; Ouchi, 1981). The creation of corporate culture requires the development of mission statements that create a frame or perceptual filter that can be used by organizational members to make sense of their experiences in the organization (Weick, 1995). A dominant discourse about corporate culture includes a homogeneous and monolithic code of behaviors for its members (Verweel, Chapter 2). Corporate culture is strengthened when meanings are constructed 'in community' because it ensures that eventually everyone will have the same viewpoint. This practice is assumed to enhance group cohesion that is exemplified by shared values and norms. The popularity of the integration perspective in managerial practices suggests therefore that the results of these case studies are neither unique to the sport situation nor to organizational practices in the Netherlands. It is possible however, that the preference for the integration perspective may be stronger in sport than elsewhere.

A functional perspective assumes that sport has various (positive) societal functions such as strengthening social integration and cohesion, as playing a role in nation building (top sport) and international relations, in enhancing health and well being, and, in providing opportunities for the safe release of tensions and frustration (Coakley, 2004). Sport is functionally defined as a democratic institution because everyone participates under the same rules and often against people of similar abilities. In some sports, such as golf and horse racing, handicaps serve to equalize the competition even more. This assumption of equal opportunity is one reason many sport administrators assume that sport is neutral with respect to social relations (Knoppers, Chapter 5). Sage (1990) argues that:

> Although sport practices embody specific and identifiable purposes, values, and meanings, they are typically viewed by both participant and spectators as a-historical and apolitical in nature ... Moreover, sport leaders tend to view themselves as impartial facilitators operating in a value-free and ideologically neutral setting (p. 11/12).

This belief in the neutrality and therefore, in the global meanings given to sport are illustrated in the case study about sport and international development. It is assumed that South African coaches can be given the same coaching education courses as Dutch coaches not only because the program in itself is excellent but also implicitly, because sport is sport, the world over; everyone plays by the same rules and uses the same skills. This is not to suggest that the integration perspective is used in a similar way in sport and nonsport organizations.

Board members in sport organizations are not the only ones who often view sport from a functionalist perspective. As Coakley (2004) points out, the functionalist discourse about sport is frequently used by the media, by scholars, by government officials at the local, national, and international levels, by national and international sport officials (and their organizations), etc. These are often stakeholders in local sport clubs and thus also provide important support for these viewpoints as the merger and the professionalization studies indicate. Athletes may view sport in a functionalist way as well; it may be the way they have been taught to make sense of sport. Possibly, they also accept the dominant functional discourses because they have very little choice if they want to participate in organized sport. Sport teams do not have a tradition of democracy and those in leadership positions in sport often act as 'soft despots' (Corlett, 1997). Most athletes are aware of who controls their sport clubs and their sport opportunities; occasionally they may protest but rarely do they do so collectively. None of the athletes involved in these case studies organized a collective form of resistance although sport administrators rarely took the meanings they assign to their sport participation seriously. Athletes frequently accepted the situation and its accompanying hegemonic discourse, let themselves be defined by it and/or dropped out. Board members are also athletes or former athletes and therefore have been socialized into this functionalist integrative paradigm as well. As a result, the use of the integration perspective in both popular ideas about management and about sport may reinforce its use and popularity among sport administrators and officials. This does not mean that world wide sport administrators use the integration perspective in the same way The preference for its use may be a global phenomenon but its contours may be specific to the context and be confounded by the ways in which sport is locally structured and the ways in which individuals in a specific context, make sense of that structure. The voluntary nature of sport organizations may also influence the way an integration perspective is used. Volunteer board members may be more inclined than managers in work organizations to work to obtain consent of its volunteer members on whose behalf they govern the club. Further research is needed to explore ways in which these dynamics may differ across context in which volunteers and paid professionals deal with differences in viewpoints and social membership.

DIFFERENTIATION

Many organizations tend to cope with diversity by emphasizing individual equality while at the same time differentiating informally between various social groups. This differentiation is formally structured in sport where competitions are organized by age, gender and by skill level. The purpose of such differentiation is to create fair competition. Thus in one sense, board members accept the necessity of differentiation within their sport clubs while at the same time they strive for integration. Such differentiation is often used to create status differences since individual club members are not treated equally. The resources and the degree of attention they receive and the value that is assigned to their performance, are in part, dependent on their social group membership. The performances of some groups are valued more than others so that they receive the most material resources. The men's best football team in a club receives more resources than the best women's team and best youth team. These differences are seen as self-evident. In other words, many club members tend to be united in their acceptance of forms of differentiation.

Sport administrators and individuals who hold an integration perspective tend to see sport as an instrument for ethnic/racial (social) integration. They often regard clubs that are formally organized on the basis of ethnicity (or of sexual preference or gender) as undesirable and as fostering social inequality (Elling & Knop, 1999; Elling, de Knop & Knoppers, 2003). These administrators may ignore the possibility that *nonimmigrant* clubs may contribute more to social inequality by marginalizing certain social groups than that they serve the interests of a diversity of individuals. Kamalo Balo is a better example of a multicultural club than are most nonimmigrant clubs, probably because it began as a Surinam club and not as a white ethnic majority club. Its incorporation was rooted in marginalized ethnicities. Although sport administrators argue that equal opportunity has no ethnicity or gender, they tend to categorize ethnic minorities and women solely as homogeneous groups. Ironically this practice strengthens group boundaries because minorities and women become very visible as tokens (Kanter, 1977). Women and ethnic minorities may be constructed as 'other' so that their presence and the salience attached to their ethnicity and gender may strengthen the identity of the majority group. In other words, their ethnic or gender identity is seen as the most salient factor of identification (Knoppers, Chapter 5; Verweel & Anthonissen, Chapter 6). The fact that everyone is simultaneously classed, gendered, ethnicized, and sexualized escapes notice. Diversity is then seen as belonging primarily to the 'other' and the privileges of the dominant group are ignored.

Sport clubs not only differentiate among members but also differ in the meanings and values that are given to individual identities. The values and status attached to "white", "heterosexual", and, "male" may be different in an European Dutch club than in a Turkish Dutch sport club. The meanings assigned to ethnicity, gender and sexual preference may vary in the ways they influence the structure of the club. In a club consisting of only female athletes, the best women's team may receive most of the material resources; a similar team in a mixed gender club tends to receive fewer resources than its male counterpart. The hierarchy of resources assigned to gender may be different again if that mixed gender club is organized primarily for gays and lesbians (Elling, de Knop & Knoppers, 2003). All sport clubs also treat members differently according to age. Consequently, although board members may intend to create a context for fair play by organizing different teams according to gender and age, at the same time, they also construct an informal hierarchy in which some teams are more valued than others. These various group identities are not just formally defined and incorporated in the statutes of club but also reflect hierarchies based on status privileges outside sport and intersect with each other (Anthonissen & Verweel, in press).

Intersections between social relations occur in every culture in both sport and nonsport settings. The localized or globalized nature of their intersection may vary by social relation. Homophobia tends to be a dominant global force in sport regardless of culture. The general societal acceptance of gays and the legal status of gay marriage in the Netherlands for example, are not reflected in Dutch sport organizations (Elling, De Knop & Knoppers, 2003; Janssen, Elling & Kalmhout, 2003). This seems to suggest that homophobia is stronger as a global force in sport than are local practices. In contrast to this globalization, gendered practices seem to be frequently localized. Football for example, is considered a men's sport in the Netherlands and a sport for both women and men in the USA (Knoppers & Anthonissen, 2004). Gendered meanings given to a sport may determine who plays it and the extent to which they are valued and allotted material resources. Thus, global and local meanings determine the resources and hierarchical status assigned to sports and teams associated with various social relations. The nature of these hierarchies may be context specific but their construction means sport administrators sustain differentiation while simultaneously striving for integration! The attempts of the actors in these case studies to erase differences fits with Martin's (1992) point that the stronger the experiences of differentiation and fragmentation within an organization, the stronger the call to do everything possible to enhance integration.

FRAGMENTATION PERSPECTIVE

The various case studies show that a reliance on an integration perspective by excluding viewpoints and status differences can be detrimental to sport organizations in many ways. Yet defining diversity only in terms of categorical social relation and/or only in terms of classless, genderless and ethnically neutral viewpoints can also limit sport organizations.

The intersections of discourses about social group relations create ambiguous and shifting social identities that are shaped by their salience in discourses about organizational processes. Sense making of diversity tends not to create coherent discourses but discourses that are ambiguous about doing sameness and doing difference (Kamp & Hagedoorn, 2004). Consequently, ambiguities are an inevitable part of the organizational processes of sport clubs although they may not always be accepted or recognized as such.

Ambiguities do not emerge suddenly as reaction to an issue, but as Verweel points out (Chapter 2), they are embedded in the initial construction of an organization or sport club and reflect intersections of social forces in sport and in the rest of society. Differences and ambiguities exist in abundance in sport clubs but are ignored or erased and assumed to be detrimental to the ways in which sport administrators want to frame processes of sense making. This avoidance of ambiguities and complexities generated by a multiplicity of meanings can have negative consequences for sport and nonsport organizations as these case studies indicate. These negative consequences have received attention in the managerial literature about sport and nonsport organizations. Space does not permit us an extensive exploration of this literature. In summary however, organizational diversity is assumed to increase creativity and innovation within the organization while also increasing ambiguity and complexity (Doherty & Chelladurai, 199; Cunningham & Sagas, 2005).

Obviously sport administrators need to be encouraged to engage in a paradigm shift from relying solely on an integration perspective to using and combining perspectives of integration, differentiation and ambiguity in an eclectic manner. The use of a fragmentation perspective requires individuals to pay attention to both social groups and individuals and to one's own role in creating meanings from which norms and values flow (Anthonissen, 2000; Siebers Verweel & de Ruijter, 2002). Use of a fragmentation perspective demands recognition of categorical groups and the status differences that accompany categorizations within a specific context, and, of differences within groups. It requires recognition and acceptance of paradoxes and of the limits and possibilities they place on agency which may be in opposition to the dominant functional perspective used to give meaning to sport. It may be much easier for sport administrators to sell sport as an instrument for integration or for nation building than as a social practice that reinforces and at times, contests inequitable social relations. It may be difficult for sport administrators (and researchers!!) to engage in self reflectivity and to acknowledge that their ways of sense making are influenced by their social positions and experiences defined by gender, ethnicity and sexual preference. Yet, as is evident in the case studies, board members in sport organizations acknowledge that change is imperative. An acceptance of ambiguity may lead to the creation of fluid meanings that transcend differences based on social groups such as age, gender, and ethnicity (see also Doherty & Chelladurai, 1999). Possibly the need for change might encourage them to value diverse ways of making sense about sport.

Most of the practices detailed in the case studies contribute to dominant processes of sense making in sport, that are associated with white masculinities. Yet, these hegemonic and often invisible processes of sense making are also leaky as is illustrated by the struggle of women to be able to participate in sport and by the efforts of immigrants to establish their own clubs although their discourses are often marginalized. Perhaps it is in the margins where playing room can be found to bring about change in many sport clubs and organizations. Those who are marginalized in sport may have the room to experiment and to develop alternate discourses because they have little vested interest in the status quo. This change, therefore, means that sport administrators need to listen to the marginalized whose voices have been missing from the dominant discourses about sport. If administrators do not make such a shift, athletes and volunteers who feel that their ways of making sense of sport are marginalized may move out of (formally) organized sport, organize their own sport experiences, and/or drop out of sport completely.[3] Listening to the marginalized means acknowledging and accepting ambiguities and differences.

The results of the case studies suggest that board members in sport organizations are aware of processes of differentiation and ambiguities within their organization but frequently do not attend to these processes because they are afraid to lose their position/power and/or do not have the tools to accept the outcomes. Possibly then, avoidance of the pitfalls that befell the actors in these case studies requires different types of leaders. It demands sport administrators who develop or have developed insight into processes of sense making.

It asks for sport administrators and officials who understand that sameness and difference are not in opposition to each other but are dialectical constructions, who encourage and value social and viewpoint diversity among athletes and sport administrators and officials, and, who coordinate the various meanings assigned to sport participation within the structure of the club with the use of open and reflective dialogue. Such leaders understand that differences have always existed and that not all differences have to be resolved (Reynolds & Trehan, 2003).

They acknowledge that the discourses they and club members use are also constructed, reinforced and/or contested by the media, by the government, by societal changes and by various other stake holders. They realize that sport is not only a half-open system with respect to economic forces but to other social forces as well. They accept that sport clubs are places where both social and viewpoint diversity exist and that acknowledging such diversity may be a sign of strength rather than a weakness that needs to be minimized or erased.

FINAL REFLECTIONS

Sense making as a tool for organizational analysis
The approach to organizational analysis was grounded in sense making. This approach acknowledges the agency of managers and administrators. It focuses on the sense maker as an individual engaging in interactions. This results show how strict adherence to an integration perspective in this sense making can have negative consequences. Since sense making is an agentic process however, the results also point to possible avenues for change. As agentic sense makers, sport administrators make choices about the frames they use to govern their club. The frames therefore are not rooted in determinism but can

be minimized. In other words, the use of sense making as an analytic tool in organizational analysis can unmask meanings. Subsequently, unmasking can yield possible avenues for action. At the same time, we acknowledge that societal structures and forces also influence the ways in which administrators make sense of situations. Sense making as an analytic tool therefore requires reflectivity on personal and societal meanings and their intersections.

Contextuality

The case studies refer to situations defined by a specific context. They represent typical dynamics in Dutch sport clubs and organizations since they represent the results of larger research studies. The results are not totally unique to the Dutch setting, however. Our comparisons of the results of the various case studies to the scholarly literature in sport and/or management have shown a considerable amount of congruencies. In addition, we have continually attempted to delineate the localized and globalized nature of our findings. The results represent dynamics that occur in many sport organizations worldwide, regardless of setting although the particularities of the dynamics may be specific to the setting. The content of the case studies can act as maps or examples for sport administrators who wish to explore various perspectives for sense making in their own sport clubs. The maps are not complete, however.

Epistemology

The case studies in this book are incomplete because they only present differing views within a particular social position. This in itself is not wrong but the use of a unitary standpoint epistemology can be problematic when it is not acknowledged and when it is assumed to be the only possible framework or to be the perspective that counts for everyone. Most of the chapters in this book are rooted in a masculinist Eurocentric perspective. This is not uncommon. As Slack (1997) argues, accounts about organizations are usually men's accounts of organizational reality. The case studies describe primarily the experiences of male board members in sport organizations, of athletes and of administrators.

The chapters describe the world of sport and its organizations as seen through the eyes of white men. This is not to say that all male board members in sport organizations think alike; examples of differences are evident throughout this book. Voices of women managers, administrators, and athletes are often missing, however. This is not surprising given that social life, including that in sport organizations, is influenced by the relative power of men and women in society and by who does the theorizing about society and sport. The viewpoints of how women experience these different situations as women are absent in all but one of the case studies. Yet these viewpoints are essential because they may in part help to create that playing room in which change can be rooted.

Other voices are missing as well. The voices of immigrants are heard only in the case study about an immigrant club. Yet, the same chapter shows that most immigrants who are involved in sport are members of nonimmigrant clubs. Where are the voices of immigrant board members in sport organizations? Similar questions can be asked about the absence of board members who are positioned differently with respect to race/ethnicity, sexual preference, age, and validity/disability. This lack of diversity of people represented in the case studies is reflected in the lack of alternate discourses among board members in sport organizations themselves. The discourses of other groups that are often marginalized in sport seem to play a minor role, if any, in establishing an alternate discourse. It would have been interesting for example, to hear the story about the football project in South Africa from several South African perspectives or that of Surinamese about nonimmigrant Dutch clubs and the way their athletes and board members in sport organizations assign meaning to their participation and to the organization. Further discussions and methods for dealing with diversity therefore, must include questions about who is doing the managing and who defines what diversity is and the extent to which social positioning influences their agency in sense making and creating different viewpoints. The power of sense making as an analytic tool can be greatly increased if administrators and managers seek out, hear and incorporate different ways of making sense in the framing of issues and solutions.

Notes

[1] Emile Durkheim (1964) was one of the first sociologists in this tradition He argued that societal cohesion is based on solidarity between members of society. He argued that common viewpoints, representations and a corresponding morality are very important to the 'proper' functioning of society. This emphasis on functioning is reflected in the name given to this paradigm: functionalism.

[2] See Cunningham & Sagas (2005) and Doherty & Chelladurai, (1999) for a brief summary of the benefits of social and cultural diversity in sport and nonsport organizations.

[3] Extreme or action sports are sites where athletes who are disillusioned with the dominant ways in which sport is organized and administered, create their own sport experiences (see for example, Wheaton, 2004).

REFERENCES

Acker, J. (1990). Hierarchies, jobs, bodies: A theory of gendered organizations. *Gender & Society*, 4, 139-158.

Acker, J. (1992). Gendering organizational theory. In A.J. Mills & P. Tancred (Eds.), *Gendering organizational analysis* (pp. 248-262). Newbury Park, CA: Sage.

Acker, J. (2000). Revisiting class: Thinking from gender, race and organizations. *Social Politics*, 7, 192-214.

Anthonissen, A. (1997). *Vitaliseringprocessen in de voetbalclub PTP* [Processes of vitalization in the football club PTP]. Utrecht: CBM

Anthonissen, A. (2000). Managerial work in sports. In M. Gastelaars (Ed.), *On Location: The relevance of the here and now in organizations* (pp. 123-144). Maastricht, The Netherlands: Shaker.

Anthonissen, A. (2001). Dutch sport organisations in transition: Organizing diversity. In J. Steenbergen, P. De Knop & A. Elling (Eds.), *Values and norms in sport: Critical reflections on the position and meanings of sport in society* (pp. 197-216). Oxford: Meyer and Meyer.

Anthonissen, A. (2004). Hybride Identificaties [Hybrid identifications]. In R. Kunnen (Ed.), *Sport in beweging. Transformatie, betekenis en kwaliteit* (pp. 61-75). Nieuwegein/Den Bosch, The Netherlands: Arko/ Mulier Instituut.

Anthonissen, A. & Boessenkool, J. (1998). *Betekenissen van besturen: Variaties in bestuurlijk handelen in amateur sport organisaties* [Meanings of management: Diversity in management of amateur sport organisations]. Utrecht: Isor.

Anthonissen, A. & Van Eekeren, F. (2000). *Interculturalisatie: Nieuwe kansen in de sport* [Interculturalism: New possibilities in sport]. Utrecht: The city of Utrecht.

Applebaum, B. (2002). Locating oneself: Self 'I' identification and the trouble with moral agency. In *Philosophy of Education* Yearbook 2001 (pp. 412 - 422). Retrieved on January 21, 2005 from http://www.ed.uiuc.edu/EPS/PES-yearbook/2001.

Bailey, F.G. (1977). *Morality and expediency: The folklore of academic politics*. Oxford: Basil Blackwell.

Barth, F. (Ed.) (1969). *Ethnic groups and boundaries: The social organization of cultural difference*. London: George Allan and Unwin.

Benschop, Y. (1996). *De mantel der gelijkheid: Gender in organisaties* [The coat of equality: Gender in organizations]. Assen, NL: Van Gorcum.

Bissett, N. (2004). Diversity writ large: Forging the link between diverse people and diverse organisational possibilities. *Journal of Organizational Change Management*, 17(3), 315-325.

Blommaert, J. (1995). Ideologies in intercultural communication. In. O. Dahl (Ed.), *Intercultural communication and contact* (pp. 9-27). Stavanger: Misjonshogskolens Fortlag.

Boessenkool, J., Van De Spek, M. & Anthonissen, A. (1997). Voetbalverenigingen en fusie [Football clubs and mergers]. Utrecht/Zeist, NL: CBM/KNVB.

Boyle, M. & McKay, J. (1995). 'You leave your troubles at the gate': A case study of the exploitation of older women's labor and 'leisure' in sport. *Gender & Society*, 9, 556-575.

Breedveld, K. (2003). Rapportage sport 2003 [Report on sport 2003]. Den Haag: SCP.

Burgers, P. et al (1998). *Burger als ieder ander: Een advies inzake lokaal beleid en minderheden* [Citizens like everyone else: A recommendation for local policy and ethnic minorities]. Utrecht: University Utrecht.

Cahn, S. (1994) *Coming on strong: Gender and sexuality in twentieth-century women's sport*. New York: Free Press, Macmillan.

CBS (1996). Statistische jaarboek 1996 [Statistical yearbook 1996]. Voorburg: Centraal Bureau voor Statistiek.

Coakley, J. (2004). *Sport in society: Issues and Controversies* (8th ed.). London: Mc Graw Hill.

Coenen, H. (1989). *Handelingsonderzoek als exemplarisch leren* [Action research as an example of learning by doing]. Utrecht, the Netherlands: Jan van Arkel.

Connell, R.W. (1987). *Gender & power.* Stanford, California: Stanford university.

Connell, R.W. (1995). *Masculinities.* Berkeley: University of California Press.

Corlett, J. (1997). Political philosophy and the managerial class: Implications for the administration of sport. *Journal of Sport Management*, 11, 250 – 262.

Cox. T. (2001). Creating the multicultural organization. A strategy for capturing the power of diversity. San Francisco: Jossey Boss.

Cunningham, G. & Sagas, M. (2005). Access discrimination in intercollegiate athletics. *Journal of Sport and Social Issues*, 29, 148 - 163

De Maertelaar, K., Van Hoecke, J., De Knop, P., Van Heddegem, L., & Theeboom, M . (2002). Marketing in organised sport: Participation, expectations and experiences of children. *European Sport Management Quarterly*, 2, 113-134.

Deal, T. & Kennedy, A. (1982). *Corporate cultures. The rites and rituals of corporate life.* Reading, MA: Addison- Wesley.

Deem, R. (1986). *All work and no play? The sociology of women and leisure.* Milton Keynes, UK: Open University Press.

Dellinger, K. (2004). Masculinities in 'safe' and 'embattled' organizations: Accounting for pornographic and feminist magazines. *Gender & Society*, 18, 545-566.

Digel, H. & Fornhoff, P. (1989). *Sport in der Entwicklungszusammenarbeit.* [Sport in international development]. München: Weltforum-Verlag.

Doherty, A. & Chelladurai, P. (1999). Managing cultural diversity in sport organizations: A theoretical perspective. *Journal of Sport Management*, 13, 280 – 297.

Douglas, M. (1982). *Essays with sociology of perception.* London: Routledge.

Durkheim, E. (1964). *The division of labour in society.* New York: Free Press.

Duyvendak, J.W. (1998). *Integratie door sport.* [Integration through sport]. Rotterdam: Bestuursdienst Rotterdam.

Elling, A. & De Knop, P. (1999). *Naar eigen wensen en mogelijkheden*, [According to one's own wishes and possibilities]. Arnhem: NOC*NSF.

Elling, A. (2002). *"Ze zijn er niet voor gebouwd". In en uitsluiting in de sport naar sekse en etniciteit.* [They aren't build for it. Inclusion and exclusion in sport across gender and ethnicity]. Nieuwegein: Arko Press.

Elling, A. De Knop, P. & Knoppers, A . (2001). The social integrative meaning of sport: A critical and comparative analysis of policy and practice in the Netherlands. *Sociology of Sport Journal*, 20, 414-434.

Elling, A. de Knop, P. & Knoppers, A. (2003). Gay/Lesbian sport clubs and events: Places of homosocial bonding and cultural resistance. *International Review for the Sociology of Sport*, 38, 441-456.

Emancipatieraad (1997). *Sport & gender: Vrouwen in beeld* [Sport & gender: Women in the picture]. Den Haag, the Netherlands: Ministerie van Sociale Zaken, Advies en Onderzoek.

Entzinger, H. (1998). Het voorportaal van Nederland [The gateway to the Netherlands]. In K. Entzinger, H. (2004). *Integration and orientation courses in a European perspective.*

Erasmus Universiteit Rotterdam, the Netherlands: ERCOMER.

Fairclough, N. (1995). *Critical discourse analysis*. Harlow: Longman.

F.L. fails to finish a match (1995). *Utrechts Nieuwsblad*, 27 november.

Gay, P. du (1997). *Production of culture, cultures of production: Culture, media and identity*. London: Sage.

Giddens, A. (1979). *Central problems in social theory*. London: MacMillan Press.

Giddens, A. (1984). *The constitution of society*. London: Polity Press.

Glastra, F. (1996). Intercultureel management en de calculatie van verschil [Cross cultural management and the calculation of difference]. *Opleiding & Ontwikkeling*, 9, 13-20.

Glastra, F. (2001). Diversiteitsmanagement in Nederland [Diversity management in the Netherlands]. In Forum (Ed), *Het leven en de leer* (pp. 9-34). Utrecht, The Netherlands: Forum.

Hall, M.A., Cullen, D. & Slack, T. (1990). The gender structure of national sport organizations. *Sport Canada: Occasional papers*, vol. 2 (1) Ottawa, Canada: Government of Canada, Fitness and Amateur Sport

Hannerz, U. (1992). *Cultural complexity. Studies in the social organization of meaning*. New York: Colombia University Press.

Hargreaves, J. & Tomlinson, A. (1992). Getting there: Cultural theory and the sociological analysis of sport in Britain, *Sociology of Sport Journal*, 9, 207-219.

Hargreaves, J. (1994). *Sporting females. Critical issues in the history and sociology of women's sport*. London: Routledge.

Hoek, S. & Van Veen, F. (1997): Elke oogopslag, elke huidskleur, elke beweging kan kwetsend zijn. [Each eye movement, each skin color, each movement can hurt someone] *De Volkskrant*, 76, 18 October, p. 9.

Hofstede, G. (1992). *Allemaal andersdenkenden* [Everyone thinks differently]. Amsterdam: Contact.

Horch, D. (1997). Self destroying processes of sportclubs in Germany. *European Journal for Sport Management*, 1, 46-57.

Hovden, J. (2000)."Heavyweight" men and younger women? The gendering of selection processes in Norwegian sport organizations, *NORA*, 8, 17-32.

Hover, P. (2002). *Sport in cijfers*. [Sport in figures]. Arnhem: NOC*NSF.

Hylmo, A. (2004). Women, men, and changing organizations: An organizational culture examination of gendered experiences of telecommuting. In P. Buzzanell, H. Sterk & L. Turner (Eds.), *Gender in applied communication contexts* (pp. 47 -68). Thousand Oaks, CA: Sage Publishing.

Isabella, L.A. (1990). Evolving interpretations as a change unfolds: How managers construe key organizational events. *Academy of Management Journal*, 33, 1, 7-41.

Jansens, J. (1998). *Etnische tweedeling in sport* [Ethnic division in sport]. Den Bosch, The Netherlands: Diopter.

Janssens, J., Elling, A. & Kalmhout, J. Van (2003). *Het gaat om de sport. Een onderzoek naar de sportdeelname van homoseksuele mannen en lesbische vrouwen.* [Participation is most important: A study of the sport participation of gays and lesbians]. Nieuwegein/Den Bos: Arko Sports/ W.J.H. Mulier Instituut.

Kalb, D. (1997). The limits of the new social orthodoxy. *Focaal: Tijdschrift voor de Antropologie*, 30-31, 236-260.

Kamp, A. & Hagedoorn-Rasmussen, P. (2004). Diversity management in a Danish context:

Towards a multicultural or segregated working life. *Economic and Industrial Democracy*, 25, 525-554.

Kanter, R.M. (1977). *Men and women of the corporation*. New York: Basic Books.

Kearny, A.T. (1992). *Sport als inspiratiebron voor de samenleving* [Sport as source of inspiration for society]. Arnhem: NOC*NSF.

Kerfoot, D. & Knights, D. (1998). Managing masculinity in contemporary organizational life: A 'man'agerial project, *Organization*, 5, 65-89.

Kimmel, M. (1999). Masculinity as homophobia: Fear, shame and silence in the construction of gender identity. In J. Kuypers (Ed.), *Men and power* (pp. 105 - 128). NY: Amherst Books,

Kirby, E.L. & Harter, L.M. (2003). Speaking the language of the bottom line: The metaphor of managing diversity. *Journal of Business Communication*, 40, 28 –49.

Knoppers, A. & Anthonissen, A. (2001). Meanings given to performance in Dutch sport organizations; Gender and racial/ethnic subtexts, *Sociology of Sport Journal*, 18, 302-316.

Knoppers, A. & Anthonissen, A. (2003). Women's soccer in the United States and the Netherlands: Differences and similarities in regimes of inequalities. *Sociology of Sport Journal*, 20, 351-370.

Knoppers, A. & Anthonissen, A. (2005). Male athletic and managerial masculinities: Congruencies in discursive practices? *Journal of Gender Studies*.

Knoppers, A. & Bouman, Y. (1996). *Trainers/coaches: een kwestie van kwaliteit?* [Trainers / coaches: A question of equality?]. Papendal, Arnhem: NOC*NSF.

Knoppers, A. & Bouman, Y. (1998). *Altijd beter dan mijn sporters* [Always better than my athletes]. Papendal, Arnhem: NOC*NSF.

Knoppers, A. & Elling, A. (1999). *Het is leuker om zelf te voetballen: Beeldvorming over de trainersfunctie in het voetbal.* [It is more fun to play than to coach: Images of football coaches]. Zeist: KNVB.

Knoppers, A. & Elling, A. (2001). Sport and the media: Race and gender in the representation of athletes and events. In J. Steenbergen, P. De Knop & A. Elling (Eds.), *Values and norms in sport: Critical reflections on the position and meanings of sport in society* (pp. 281-300). Aachen: Meyer & Meyer Sport.

Knoppers, A. & Elling, A. (2004). "We don't do promotional journalism": Discursive strategies used by sport journalists to describe the selection process. *International Review for the Sociology of Sport*, 39, 55-71.

Knoppers, A. (1992). Explaining male dominance and sex segregation in coaching. Three perspectives. *Quest*, 44, 210-227.

Koot, W. & Hogema, I. (1992). *Organisatiecultuur: Fictie en werkelijkheid* [Organizational culture: Fiction and reality]. Muiderberg: Coutinho.

Koski, P. & Heikkala, J. (1997). Professionalization and organization of mixed rationales: The case of Finnish national sport organizations. *European Journal for Sport Management*, 1, 7-29.

Lagendijk, E. & Van de Gugten, M. (1996). *Sport en allochtonen.* [Sport and immigrants]. Rijswijk: Ministerie van VWS.

Latour, B. (1994). *Wij zijn nooit modern geweest. Pleidooi voor een symmetrische antropologie* [We were never modern: Plea for a symmetrical anthropology]. Rotterdam: Van Gennep.

Lorber, J. (1993). Believing is seeing: Biology as ideology. *Gender & Society*, 7, 568-581.

Macintosh, D. & Whitson, D. (1990). *The game planners: Transforming Canada's sport system*. Montreal: McGill – Queens University Press.

Maguire, J. (1999). *Global sport: Identities, societies, civilizations*. Cambridge: Polity Press.

Martin, J. (1992). *Cultures in organizations. Three perspectives*. New York: Oxford University Press.

Martin, J. (2002). *Organizational culture. Mapping the terrain*, London: Sage.

Mastenbroek, W.F.G. (2002). *Conflicthantering en organisatie ontwikkeling* [Dealing with conflict in organizational development]. Alphen a/d Rijn, the Netherlands: Samson.

Mc Carthy, D. & Jones, R.L. (1997). Speed, aggression, strength and tactical naiveté: The portrayal of the black soccer player on the television. *Journal of Sport and Social Issues*, 21, 4, 348-362.

McKay, J. (1997). *MANaging gender*. Albany: State University of New York Press.

McKay, J. (1999) Gender and organizational power in Canadian sport. In P. White & K. Young (Eds.), *Sport and gender in Canada* (pp. 197-213). Oxford: University Press,

McPhee, R. & Zaug, P. (2001). Organizational theory, organizational communication, organizational knowledge, and problematic integration. *Journal of Communication*, 51, 574- 591.

Memorandum of Understanding (1994). Rijswijk, The Netherlands: Ministerie van VWS.

Messner, M. (1988). Sport and male domination: The female athlete as contested ideological terrain. *Sociology of Sport Journal*, 5, 197-211.

Messner, M. (1992). *Power at play: Sports and the problem of masculinity*. Boston: Beacon Press.

Messner, M. (2002). *Taking the field. Women, men and sport*. Minneapolis: University of Minnesota Press.

Meyerson, D. & Kolb, D. (2000). Moving out of the armchair: Developing a framework to bridge the gap between feminist theory and practice. *Organization*, 7, 553-571.

Moodley, R. (1999). "Masculine/managerial masks and the 'other' subject. In S.M. Whitehead & R. Moodley (Eds.), *Transforming managers: Gendering change in the public sector* (pp. 214-233). New York; Routledge

Moore, M.E., Parkhouse, B.L. & Konrad, A.M. (2001). Women in sport management: Advancing the representation through HRM structures. *Women in Management Review*, 16, 51-61.

Nederveen Pieterse, J. (1996). Globalisation and culture: Three paradigms. *Economic and Political Weekly*, 23, 1389-1393.

Nier, O. & Sheard, K. (1999). Managing change: The economic, social and symbolic dimensions of professionalisation in five elite European rugby clubs. *European Journal of Sport Management*, 2, 5-33.

O'Brien, D. & Slack, T. (1999). Deinstitutionalising the amateur ethic: An empirical examination of change in Rugby Union Football *Sport Management Review*, 2, 24-42.

Ouchi, W. (1978). Markets, bureaucracies and clans. *Administrative Science Quaterly*, 25, 129-141.

Parker, M. (2000). *Organizational culture and identity*. London: Sage

Pascoe, C. (2003). Multiple masculinities? Teenager boys talk about jocks and gender. *American Behavioural Scientist*, 46, 1423-1438.

Pauw, V. (2000). *Coed soccer*. Unpublished paper. Zeist, the Netherlands: KNVB,

Department Girls and women's soccer.

Peters, T. & Waterman, R. (1982). *In search of excellence*. New York: Harper and Row.

Prasad, P. Mills, A. Elmes, M. & Prasad, A. (Eds) (1997) *Managing the organizational melting pot. Dilemmas of workplace diversity*. London: Sage.

Pronk J. & Terpstra, E. (1998). *Sport in ontwikkeling: Samenspel scoort!* [Sport in development: Teamwork scores!). Den Haag, the Netherlands: Ministerie van Buitenlandse Zaken en Ministerie van VWS.

Putnam, R.D. (2000). *Bowling alone. The collapse and revival of American community*. New York: Simon & Schuster

Raivo, M. (1986). The life and careers of women in leading positions in Finnish sport organizations. In J. Mangan & R. Small (Eds.), *Sport, culture, society: International perspectives* (pp. 270- 280). London: E & F Spon.

Rapport Integratie Beleid Minderheden. [Rapport Integration Policy for Immigrants (2003). Den Haag, The Netherlands: SCP.

Reskin, B. (1988). Bringing the men back in: Sex differentiation and the devaluation of women's work. *Gender & Society*, 2, 58-81.

Reynolds, M. & Trehan, K. (2003). Learning from difference? *Management Learning*, 34, 163-176.

Roosevelt, T.R. (1993). Managing diversity. In Anne Frank stichting (Ed.), *De multiculturele organisatie en het belang van intercultureel management* [The multicultural organization and the importance of intercultural management]. Deventer: Kluwer.

Ruijter, A. de (1995). Cultural pluralism and citizenship. *Culture Dynamics*, 7, 215-232.

Sage, G. (1990). *Power and ideology in American sport: A critical perspective*. Champaign, IL.: Human Kinetics.

Schenk, H. (1996). Fuseren en innoveren [Mergers and innovations]. *Economisch statistische Berichten*, 8, 248-252.

Siebers, H., Verweel, P. & Ruijter, A. de (2002). *Management van diversiteit in arbeidsorganisaties*. [Management of diversity in work organizations]. Utrecht, the Netherlands: Lemma

Slack, T. (1997). *Understanding sport organizations*. Champaign, IL.: Human Kinetics.

Sociaal en Cultureel Rapport 1998 [Social and Cultural Report 1998]. The Hague, The Netherlands: Sociaal Cultureel Planbureau.

Steenbergen, J. & Tamboer, J.W.I (1998). Ethics and the double character of sport: An attempt to systematize the discussion on the ethics of sport. In M.J. Mc Namee & S.J. Parry (Eds.), *Ethics and sport* (pp. 35-53). London: E& FN Spon.

Steenbergen, J. (2004). *Grenzen aan de sport* [Limitations of sport]. Maarssen: Elsevier.

Stol, P. (1995). *Speurtocht gewenst: Vrouwelijke trainers!* [A search is needed: Women coaches!] Internship report. Utrecht, the Netherlands; Universiteit Utrecht, Tracé Sport, Bewegen en Gezondheid, vakgroep Pedagogiek. .

Swank, M. (1996). *Voetbalvereniging F.L* [Football club F. L.]. Utrecht, the Netherlands: CBM, Universiteit Utrecht.

Swank, M. & Van Eekeren, F. (1998). *Sport en ontwikkelingssamenwerking. Verslag van het symposium*. [Sport and international development: A symposium report]. Utrecht: CBM and DVL/OS.

Tennekes, J. (1995). *Organisatiecultuur: een antropologische visie* [Organizational culture: An anthropological perspective]. Leuven/Apeldoorn: Garant.

Timmer, B (1995). *Als vrouwen willen voetballen, willen ze ook coachen* [When women play football, they also want to coach it] . Afstudeerproject, CMV: Vrouw en Welzijn, Hogeschool de Horst, Driebergen, the Netherlands.

Tolson, A. (1996). *Mediations: Text and discourses in media studies.* Arnold Publishing Co.

Trice, H.M. & Beyer, J.M. (1993). *The culture of work organizations.* Englewood Cliffs/New Yersey: Prentice Hall.

Van Dale Groot woordenboek der Nederlandse Taal [Van Dale dictionary of the Dutch language]. Den Haag: Martinus Nijhoff.

Van De Brink, G. (1978). Ideologie en hegemonie bij Gramsci [Ideology and hegemony according to Gramsci]. In H. Boekraad & H. Hoeks (Eds.), *Te elfe ure* (pp. 10-58). Nijmegen, the Netherlands: Socialistic Publisher.

Van de Meulen, R.. (2003). Betrokkenheid: volgers, toeschouwers en vrijwilligers. [Involvement: Fans, spectators and volunteers]. In K. Breedveld (Ed.), *Rapportage Sport 2003* (pp. 99-124). Den Haag, The Netherlands: SCP.

Van Eekeren, F. (1997). *Coach the coaches. Onderzoek naar een sportontwikkelingsproject in Zuid-Afrika* [Coach the coaches: Researching a sport project in South Africa]. Utrecht: CBM, University Utrecht.

Van Eekeren, F. (2001).*Visieontwikkeling platform Sport en Ontwikkelingssamenwerking.* [Platform for strategic planning in sport and international cooperative development]. Utrecht: BDW Advies.

Van Sterkenburg, J. & Knoppers, A. (2004). Dominant discourses about race/ethnicity and gender in sport practice and performance. *International Review for the Sociology of Sport,* 39, 301-321.

Vermeulen, H. & Penninx, R. (2000). *Immigrant integration.* Amsterdam: Het spinhuis.

Verweel, P. (1987). *Universiteit: Verandering en planning.* [University: Changing and planning]. Icau mededelingen no.28, Utrecht: SWP.

Verweel, P. (2000). *Betekenisgeving in organisatiestudies. De mechanisering van het sociale.* [Meaning in organizational studies: Mechanisation of the social]. Utrecht, The Netherlands: Isor.

Verweel, P. (2001). Bewogen gewogen: beschouwingen over multiculturalisme. [Moved weight: views of multiculturalism]. In Forum, *Het leven en de leer* (pp. 35-42). Deventer: Salland de Lange.

Verweel, P. & David, K. (1995). *Verborgen dimensies: cultuur en macht in fusies* [Hidden dimensions: Culture and power in mergers). Utrecht: SWP.

Verweel, P. & David, K.(1995). *Beeld en zelfbeeld van een allochtone vereniging.* [Image and image of an immigrant club]. Utrecht: CBM, Universiteit Utrecht.

Vink, N. & Schapink, D. (1994). Lerende organisaties in ontwikkelingssamenwerking *[Changing organizations in international development].* In W. Koot & J. Boessenkool (Eds.), *Management & Organisatie [Management & Organization] thema Intercultureel Management,* [theme Intercultural Management]. Alphen aan de Rijn: Samson.

Wajcman, J. (1998). *Managing like a man: Women and men in corporate management.* University Park, PA: Pennsylvania State University Press.

Ward, J. & Winstanley, D. (2003) The absent presence: Negative space within discourse and the construction of minority sexual identity in the workplace. *Human Relations,* 56 (10), pp. 1255+

Weick, K. (1995). *Sense making in organizations.* London: Sage Publications.

*Weick, K. (2001). *Making sense of the organization*. Malden, Massachusetts, USA; Blackwell Business.

Wheaton, B. (Ed.) (2004). Understanding lifestyle sports: consumption, identity and difference. London: Routledge.

White, A. & Brackenridge, C. (1985). Who rules sport? Gender divisions in the power structure of British sport organizations from 1960. *International Review for the Sociology of Sport*, 20, 96 - 107.

Whitehead, S. (2002). *Men and masculinities*. Cambridge UK: Polity Press.

Whitehead, S.M. & Barrett, F.J. (2001). The sociology of masculinity. In S.M. Whitehead & F.J. Barrett (Eds.), *The masculinities reader* (pp. 30-50). Cambridge, UK: Polity Press.

Zoonen L. van (1998). A professional, unreliable, heroic marionette (M/F): Structure, agency and subjectivity in contemporary journalisms. *European Journal of Cultural Studies*, 1, 123-143.

PROFILES

All of the authors are (former) athletes. Currently they are faculty members at the Utrecht School of Governance, University of Utrecht in the Netherlands.

Anton Anthonissen is researcher in the area of diversity in (sport) organizations. He did several research projects for governmental organizations and national sport organizations that focused on diversity, etnicity, gender, sport and management/governance. He is program director of the master sport policy and sport management at the Utrecht School of Governance.

Jan Boessenkool has studied sport through the lens of an organizational anthropologist. He has been involved in various projects in countries in Africa for ten years. His research focuses on the management and organization of sport clubs and on international cooperative development.

Frank van Eekeren is an organizational consultant and researcher who views sport organizations through the lens of intercultural management and international cooperative development. Currently he explores processes of multi-culturalism in sport. He is a member of the board of directors of the Foundation for African Sports Development (FASD) and works as a volunteer at a football club.

Annelies Knoppers is a sociologist and researcher in the area of gender and (sport) organizations. She has conducted research in the USA and the Netherlands that explores the images that athletes and coaches have of coaches, the gendering of sport media coverage, and the meanings managers give to physicality, their work and diversity.

Paul Verweel, chair of the Utrecht School for Governance, is an organizational anthropologist. His areas of expertise include diversity in organizations, strategic management, organizational culture, and the construction of meaning. He is a member of various local and national advisory boards of sport organizations.

THE BUSINESS OF SPORTS

The Business of Sports, Volume 1
Allan Edwards/James Skinner
Sport Empire

The book critizises the globalisation of sport from an Autonomist Marxist perspective. This analysis is supported by numerous international sport examples that highlight how sport is being governed by a select group of sport organisations, multinational companies and media conglomerates. This domination of the sport industry is marginalising disadvantaged groups and is subsequently being challenged by new methods of protest and resistance. "The Sport Empire" provides compelling reading for those interested in the effects of globalisation of sport.

192 pages, 3 illustrations, 3 charts
Paperback, 6^1/2" x 9^1/4"
ISBN 1-84126-168-8
$ 19.95 US/$ 29.95 CDN
c. £ 14.95 UK/€ 18.95

This Sport Management Book Series aims to incorporate cutting edge work which is designed to transcend the boundaries between business and sport.

The series will be used as a forum for research and scholarly insight surrounding the major issues of importance for those concerned with sport management and sport marketing.

The series will provide an opportunity to illustrate and highlight the ways in which the business of sport has expanded to become a global industry.

MEYER
&MEYER
SPORT

MEYER & MEYER distribution@m-m-sports.com• www.m-m-sports.com